ABC
TIME TIPS

A B C
TIME TIPS

Merrill Douglass

Illustrated by Gary Wigley

McGRAW-HILL

New York   San Francisco   Washington, D.C.   Auckland   Bogotá
Caracas   Lisbon   London   Madrid   Mexico City   Milan
Montreal   New Delhi   San Juan   Singapore
Sydney   Tokyo   Toronto

Library of Congress Cataloging-in-Publication Data

Douglass, Merrill E.
    ABC time tips / Merrill Douglass : illustrations by Gary Wigley.
      p. cm.
    ISBN 0-07-021995-8
    1. Time management.   I. Title.
HD69.T54D678   1998
650.1—dc21   97-42113
                                            CIP

McGraw-Hill

A Division of The **McGraw·Hill** Companies

1 2 3 4 5 6 7 8 9 0   DOC/DOC   9 0 3 2 1 0 9 8

ISBN 0-07-021995-8

*The sponsoring editor for this book was Betsy Brown, the editing supervisor was Jane Palmieri,
the designer was Michael Mendelsohn of MM Design 2000, Inc., and the production
supervisor was Tina Cameron. It was set in Stone Informal by MM Design 2000, Inc.*

Printed and bound by R.R. Donnelley & Sons Company.

McGraw-Hill books are available at special quantity discounts to use as premiums and
sales promotions, or for use in corporate training programs. For more information,
please write to the Director of Special Sales, McGraw-Hill, 11 West 19th Street,
New York, NY 10011. Or contact your local bookstore.

This book is printed on recycled, acid-free paper
containing a minimum of 50% recycled, de-inked
fiber.

Dedicated to

Donna Douglass

because this is the first book about managing

time that she has not helped me write, and

therefore the first chance I've had to

dedicate a book to a great wife,

mother, and coauthor.

CONTENTS

Introduction   xi

ANALYZING *Finding out where your time goes*   1

ATTITUDES *Developing positive time attitudes*   4

BALANCE *Achieving a balanced life*   6

BOSSES *Helping your boss help you*   8

BREAKS *Building breaks into your schedule*   10

CALENDARS *Making the best use of your calendar*   12

CHANGE *Responding successfully to change*   14

CLUTTER *Cleaning up the clutter around you*   16

COMMUNICATION *Improving communication to save time*   20

COMMUTING *Making the most of commuting time*   22

COMPUTER CLUTTER *Keeping junk out of your computer*   24

COMPUTERS *Using the computer to save time*   26

CRISES *Reducing crises in your job*   28

DELEGATION *Delegating effectively to gain time*   31

DESK *Managing the top of your desk*   37

DETAILS *Staying on top of all the details*   39

DICTATION *Dictating like an expert every time*   42

DISTRACTIONS *Reducing distractions in your work place*   44

DROP-INS *Minimizing the impact of drop-in visitors*   46

EFFICIENCY *Being both efficient and effective*   49

ELECTRONIC MAIL *Mastering your electronic mailbox* 51

ENERGY LEVEL *Maintaining high energy levels* 53

FILING *Finding a home for your paper* 55

FORMS *Using forms to save time* 58

GOALS *Staying focused on your goals* 60

HABITS *Creating good time habits* 62

HOME *Saving time at home* 64

HURRY *Curing yourself of hurryitis* 67

IMPROVING *Improving everything you do* 69

INDECISION *Learning to make timely decisions* 71

INFORMATION *Staying on top of information* 73

INTERRUPTIONS *Minimizing constant interruptions* 75

JOB ANALYSIS *Discovering what you actually do* 79

KILLING TIME *Thinking about timewasters* 80

LISTS *Making lists work better* 81

MAIL *Developing a systematic approach* 83

MASTER LIST *Keeping track of all your jobs* 85

MEETINGS (Before) *Preparing for productive meetings* 88

MEETINGS (During) *Conducting productive meetings* 91

MEETINGS (After) *Following up after meetings* 94

MEMORY *Remembering things when you should* 95

MORNING ROUTINE *Getting a head start on the day* 97

MYTHS *Identifying false assumptions* 99

NOTEBOOK PLANNERS *Using notebook planners effectively* 101

NOTES *Developing a standard approach* 104

OPEN-DOOR POLICY *Rethinking your open-door policy* 106

ORGANIZING *Getting better organized*   108

PAPERWORK *Streamlining your paperwork*   109

PERFECTIONISM *Overcoming perfectionistic tendencies*   113

PERSONAL *Using both sides of your brain*   115

PLANNING *Planning work and time to get ready for good results*   118

PRIORITIES *Clarifying your priorities*   124

PROCRASTINATION *Learning to do it now*   127

PROJECTS *Mastering project details*   130

QUESTIONS *Asking good questions to save time*   134

QUIET TIME *Creating noninterrupted time*   136

QUOTES *Thinking about time*   138

READING *Reading more in less time*   141

SAYING NO *Saying no positively and effectively*   145

SCHEDULING *Making time for important work*   147

SECRETARIES *Working well with secretaries and assistants*   151

SIMPLIFYING *Simplifying your life*   154

SLEEP *Making sure you get adequate rest*   158

SOCIALIZING *Maintaining a reasonable balance*   160

STAFF *Making good use of our time together*   162

STRESS *Reducing the effects of pressure, tension, and stress*   165

TEAMWORK *Improving team time and getting more done together*   169

TELEPHONES *Taming your telephone*   172

TELEPHONE TAG *Minimizing the problem of telephone tag*   177

TICKLER FILES *Mastering the power of tickler files*   179

TRAVEL *Making good use of travel time*   181

URGENCY *Avoiding the tyranny of the urgent*   185

VALUE *Understanding the value of time*   186

VISITORS *Controlling drop-in visitors who waste your time*   188

VOICE MAIL *Using voice mail effectively*   190

WAITING *Making good use of waiting time*   193

WASTEBASKETS *Using your wastebasket like a pro*   195

WRITING *Saying more with fewer words in less time*   196

eXTRAS *Maintaining your perspective*   201

YOU *Being the best you can be*   203

ZANIES *Saving time with creativity*   206

Appendix   208

Meet the Author   209

INTRODUCTION

Come on in...the water's fine!

Time is a paradox: you never seem to have enough time, yet you have all the time there is. The problem is not a shortage of time, but how you choose to use the time available.

If you're like many people these days, you've probably read something about time management and maybe even attended a time management seminar. You've probably developed some good time habits, and you're doing several things right. Yet, you're still having problems with time.

This book will help you fine-tune your time skills, build on your strengths, and create more good time habits. Think of this as an advanced manual for time management, ready to take you to the next mastery level. You'll find it a highly practical guide to mastering every aspect of time.

In 1972 I set out to change the way people think about time. Since then, I've presented over 3000 time management seminars, authored 10 time management books, recorded 24 tapes, written hundreds of magazine and newspaper articles, and broadcast over 500 radio commentaries.

This book is a collection of the best tips and techniques that have proven effective over the years. Each one has been condensed to make this the quickest- and easiest-to-read time management book ever. At the same time, it's also the most comprehensive.

This is more of a browsing book than a reading book. Keep a pen handy as you go through the pages. Check each item you want to act on. The more you use these ideas, the better they'll work for you.

Best wishes for your success as you seek to fine-tune your time management habits.

MERRILL DOUGLASS

ANALYZING

**The way you *think* you spend
your time and the way you *actually*
spend your time are rarely the same.
Don't guess, make sure you know.**

☑ The key to managing time well is to make sure your activities are consistent with your goals...that they will help you achieve your intended results. Everything you do either helps you or hinders you.

☑ Ask yourself often: "Will what I'm doing, or about to do, help me achieve my goals?" Once your time is spent, it can't be recovered.

☑ Ask others to tell you how you waste your time or how you might use your time more effectively. They see things about you that you will never see.

☑ Good time management is a systematic way of thinking and working. It requires that you constantly analyze what you are doing and look for ways to improve.

☑ Keep a record of how you really spend your time for 2 to 4 weeks every year. A month is usually best. The first three days are tough; after that, it becomes part of your daily routine. See Time Log sheet opposite.

☑ Ask questions to help analyze your time log: What problems do you see? What habits, patterns, or tendencies do you see? Was the first hour of the day productive? What was the most productive time of the day? How much time was spent on high priority items? What were the biggest timewasters?

☑ Worth getting: *Time Mastery Profile*, published by Carlson Learning Company, available from Time Management Center, 1401 Johnson Ferry Road, Suite 328, Marietta, GA 30062; 770-973-3977. In 15 to 20 minutes this instrument will identify your time management strengths and weaknesses and help you design a plan for improvement.

TIME LOG

TIME	ACTIVITY-DESCRIPTION	IMP ABC	URG ABC	INTERRUPTIONS		
				T	V	COMMENT
		ABC	ABC			
		ABC	ABC			
		ABC	ABC			
		ABC	ABC			
		ABC	ABC			
		ABC	ABC			
		ABC	ABC			
		ABC	ABC			
		ABC	ABC			
		ABC	ABC			
		ABC	ABC			
		ABC	ABC			
		ABC	ABC			
		ABC	ABC			
		ABC	ABC			
		ABC	ABC			
		ABC	ABC			
		ABC	ABC			
		ABC	ABC			
		ABC	ABC			
		ABC	ABC			
		ABC	ABC			
		ABC	ABC			
		ABC	ABC			
		ABC	ABC			
		ABC	ABC			
		ABC	ABC			
		ABC	ABC			
		ABC	ABC			

ATTITUDES

**When you approach something
with a positive attitude,
things generally work out better.**

☑ Recognize that you face a daily dilemma: too much to do and not enough time to do it. Instead of simply working faster or working longer, try working smarter.

☑ Some of your time will inevitably be wasted by events and people beyond your control. Don't fret about it. Learn to control the controllable and allow for the uncontrollable.

☑ No one can control all the events in a day, but anyone can control his or her response to those events.

☑ Dr. Norman Vincent Peale taught that attitudes are formed by the words we use when we talk to ourselves. Talk positively, and you develop positive attitudes; talk negatively, and you develop negative attitudes.

☑ Listening to 60-cycle music produces a relaxing brain wave, which makes you more susceptible to positive thoughts. The book *Superlearning* by Sheila Ostrander and Nancy Schroeder (Dell, 1979) lists hundreds of classical compositions that qualify.

☑ Laughter helps maintain positive thoughts. Listen to funny cassette tapes. Try the *Executive Humor* tape series from Nightingale-Conant Corporation (7200 North Lehigh, Chicago, IL 60611; 800-323-5552).

☑ Listen to humorous tapes as you commute. Laugh all the way to work and you may have a far more productive day.

☑ Managing time really means managing yourself. If your time is out of control, it means you are out of control. If you don't manage yourself, you relinquish control of your day to other people and random events.

☑ When facing a new idea, don't jump to criticize as most people do. First, look for all the positives; then, consider the possibilities; and, finally, think about any problems associated with it. This approach will yield far more good ideas.

☑ Managing yourself requires self-discipline. Don't think about it; don't talk about it; just do it.

☑ The key to self-discipline is simply doing what you know you should do, whether you feel like doing it or not. Doing what you feel like doing will never develop self-discipline.

BALANCE

Time is more than just a work issue; it's also a life issue. The way you spend your time defines the life you live.

☑ The way you spend your time is the way you live. If you want a different life, you'll have to spend your time differently. What changes do you need to make?

☑ Keep a personal time log for a month to find out where all your nonwork time goes. Study the record to decide what changes should be made.

☑ Think about where you get satisfaction from living. How much time do you spend on those things? How could you spend more?

☑ Many of us spend more time on the C's of life than on the A's of life. Don't allow trivial things to crowd out the important ones. Drop unimportant activities.

☑ The key to a balanced life is spending an adequate amount of time in all aspects of your life: spiritual, family, community, social, career, mental, health, leisure. Keep a personal time log to find out how your life–time is allocated. What parts of your life get too much time? Where do you need more time? How might you achieve a better balance?

☑ Live for now. All time is real time. Don't postpone your life waiting for someday to arrive.

☑ Write a personal mission statement for yourself, describing the person you intend to be.

☑ Write long-range personal goals and assign priorities to them.

☑ Minimize television in your life. The average American watches too much. Keep a record of your viewing habits for several days and decide for yourself. Ask yourself if there is something more exciting you could do with your life than watching TV.

☑ Make a list of 100 things you could do to improve your life. Start doing them.

☑ Ask yourself: "What do I wish I had more time for?" Develop an action plan for making it happen.

☑ The best use of your time is not necessarily the same as for someone else. A timewaster for you may not be a timewaster for others.

BOSSES

Think of your boss as a colleague, not an adversary. Discuss goals, plans, priorities, and problems regularly.

☑ Do everything you can to make your boss look good, especially to his or her boss. And, don't waste time complaining about your boss.

☑ Realize that even good bosses with the best intentions waste subordinate time. Make sure that you and the boss both recognize that there is a problem—that the boss really is wasting your time. Maybe what needs changing is your perception.

☑ Talk usually precedes action. Nothing much happens until you talk about it. Develop an ongoing dialogue with your boss about how to use time best. Keep the lines of communication open.

☑ Bring the problem into the open. Find ways to talk about it. Approach your boss as you would your best customer.

☑ Keep a time log before you talk to the boss. If there is a problem, it will show up on the log. You now can talk about facts, not just opinions.

☑ Many bosses respond well to Gantt charts, diagrams, and flowcharts, in addition to simple conversation.

☑ Realize that the problem may not be your boss; it may be the system. Find out who can change the system.

☑ Treat your boss at least as well as your best customer. Compensate for his or her weaknesses.

☑ There's always more than one point of view. Put yourself in the boss's position and ask: "If I were the boss, what would I want from me?" Treat your boss as you'd want to be treated if you were the boss.

☑ Offer solutions whenever you discuss a problem. Don't expect your boss to have all the answers.

☑ Try to see both the strengths and weaknesses of your boss. The greater the strengths, the greater the weaknesses are likely to be. Learn to accentuate the strengths.

☑ Be patient and understanding. You may not be aware of the problems and pressures your boss has to cope with. His or her reactions may have nothing to do with you at all.

☑ Don't waste your boss's time.

BREAKS

You need both physical and psychological breaks to perform at your best.

☑ Plan time for breaks in your work routine so you can work in peak condition.

☑ Smart woodcutters don't just chop away at the trees all day long; they also take time to sharpen their axes. Do you take time to sharpen your axe, or are you just chopping away with a dull blade?

☑ Block out vacation times at the beginning of the year. Don't allow anything to displace them.

☑ Change, pressure, stress, or tension require emotional energy. The more emotional energy you have, the more stress you can handle.

☑ To fill your emotional fuel tank, you have to stop. That means saying no sometimes, which may disappoint someone else.

☑ Be careful what you do, where you go, and who you're with. Some activities, places, and people help you fill your emotional fuel tank; others drain it.

☑ Take plenty of play breaks. Do something new, go someplace you've always wanted to go, look up an old friend, do something just for fun, do something you enjoyed as a kid (fly a kite, play hopscotch, blow bubbles).

☑ Take minivacations: Think in terms of 2 to 5 minutes; 10 to 30 minutes; 1 to 3 hours; 4 to 6 hours. Make a list of activities you would enjoy for each category. Be sure you have some fun things in all the time spans. If you can't think of anything you'd like to do in the little time spans, you probably don't have enough fun in your life.

CALENDARS

Put personal items and work items on the same calendar.

☑ Use only one calendar. If you have two calendars, you never know for sure what your commitments and schedules really are. It's like the old Chinese proverb: "The man with two clocks never knows for sure what time it is."

☑ Put personal and work things on the same calendar: one life, one calendar. Otherwise, the personal side of your life will tend to get reduced.

☑ Set criteria for what to record on your monthly calendar. What kinds of activities should you write in the daily blocks? You may find it easier to write only those activities that require your physical attendance at a particular place. Other items, like due dates and notices can be put somewhere else, such as the margin of the calendar.

☑ If you travel a lot, be sure your secretary or assistant has a duplicate of your calendar. Keep that person's calendar updated daily.

☑ A master calendar at home can help keep everyone on time, and reveal conflicts between schedules early enough to resolve them satisfactorily. It can also be used to indicate revolving household chores.

☑ The best place to keep a master calendar at home is in the kitchen.

☑ Use color coding on your calendar to indicate different kinds of items or to make some items stand out.

CHANGE

Change can either develop you or destroy you, depending on how you respond to the change.

☑ About half the people enjoy change; about half do not. Don't make people feel guilty for not instantly embracing change.

☑ Resistance is normal. Expect it; allow for it; even encourage it. Ask people to tell you all the potential problems they see and to express their concerns and fears. Don't expect all of them to be rational.

☑ Change is the greatest component of stress. The faster the changes, the greater the stress. Learn to flow with the changes in your life.

☑ Don't arbitrarily impose change without seeking lots of input from the people affected by the change. Don't spring surprises on them.

☑ Treat people like adults. Don't lie or try to con them. Tell people why the change is necessary.

☑ Let people affected by the change participate in creating the change. Allow as much autonomy as possible.

☑ Start early. Take as much time as necessary to discuss all aspects of the change before it happens. The more people know about the change, the more comfortable they will be with the change. Allow people time to adjust. Some need more time than others.

☑ Remember, there is more than one way to do anything. There may even be several "right" ways to do it.

☑ Maintain stabilizing forces in some parts of your life to offset changes in other parts.

☑ Focus on the emotional aspects of the change as much as the structural aspects.

☑ Be sure to change the reward system so it matches the new conditions. Reward appropriate risk-taking and innovation.

☑ Share the credit for success with everyone involved. Emphasize joint effort.

☑ When new management takes over at work, tell them you really want to be on their team. Be sure to act like you mean it, too.

☑ When you get a new boss, ask yourself: "What can I do to make the boss look like a winner?" Do it.

CLUTTER

Clean up clutter. It diverts your attention, hampers your thinking, dilutes your effort, and hinders your progress.

☑ When you start cleaning off your desk, don't allow yourself to get sidetracked. Stick to the task at hand.

☑ About 80 percent of the stuff in your desk drawers can safely be tossed out.

☑ No matter how great you are, you can only work on one significant thing at a time. Anything else on your desk is a source of potential distraction.

☑ Douglass's Law of Clutter: Clutter expands to fill the space available for its retention.

☑ The longer you wait to throw something out, the longer the list of excuses to prevent you from ever throwing it out.

☑ Don Aslett: "Clutter accumulates so quietly and insidiously, so gradually, we usually don't even know it has."

(*Not for Packrats Only: How to Clean Up, Clear Out, and Live Clutter-Free Forever,* Plume, 1991)

☑ Follow the 4R approach to ridding your life of clutter: recognize, repent, remove, refrain. Recognize that clutter is bad. Repent by admitting that clutter is killing you. Remove all the clutter around you. Refrain from letting clutter return.

☑ You can start either by tackling the worst spots first—or by tackling the easiest spots first. Good starting places might be your Rolodex, your center desk drawer, or maybe the hard drive on your computer.

☑ When you start cleaning up clutter, look at everything. Look in every drawer, on every shelf, in every closet or storage space. If you spot an item that has no current purpose or value, it is probably clutter.

☑ Don't move clutter to a different storage space; throw it out. Clutter is clutter no matter where it is.

☑ For sentimental items: Put them in a scrapbook; create an historical display or archive museum; frame them for display; give them away as gifts; turn them into something useful; recycle the best part of them.

☑ The more clutter around you, the more people will judge you in negative ways.

☑ To cut down on magazine clutter, tear out articles you want to read, staple the pages together, and throw out the rest of the magazine. If you haven't done anything with the torn-out articles in two months, throw them away.

☑ Don't keep books just because they are books. Books are not automatically valuable; they're only one way to bind sheets of paper together. Don't keep them if they produce no value for you. Give them away, take them to libraries, or take them to used-book shops.

☑ You can have your name removed from any mailing list by writing to the Direct Mail Marketing Association, 6 East 43rd Street, New York, NY 10017. Ask for their free "mail preference" form.

☑ Clean up your clutter when no one else is around. Kibitzers cause you to give things a second thought, which leads to a second chance, which adds to the pile of clutter. It's best to work alone.

☑ You don't need hours to start cleaning up clutter. Even a few minutes at a time will work wonders. In only a few minutes you can clean out one drawer or one bookshelf.

☑ Here's a good way to clean out drawers: (1) Dump everything out. (2) Wash, dust, or wipe it out. (3) Put back a few things you actually use. (4) Throw the rest away.

☑ Start your decluttering effort in one spot. It's easier to identify and throw away junk if you drag the junky drawer to a clean spot rather than trying to clean out the drawer in the midst of a mess. Gradually expand the cleaned-out area.

☑ Pick a place for everything, and put things in their right place. Use lots of boxes and containers. Be sure to label everything you put in a box. You shouldn't have to open a box to see what's inside.

☑ Don't keep something just because you paid good money for it. Junk is junk. Money spent on junk is simply gone.

Keeping the item around won't improve anything. Cut your losses and toss it out, or sell it if you can. Try to learn something in the process about future purchases.

☑ Don't use these common excuses: "I might need it some-day; I paid good money for this; I'm going to fix it some day; it isn't worn out yet; it's never been used; these are memories."

☑ Learn to look at empty tables or shelves and consider them okay. Just because you could pile something on it doesn't mean you should pile something on it. The empty look is great.

COMMUNICATION

The greatest myth of communication is the belief that it exists.

☑ Paraphrase people's comments to be sure you understand.

☑ Use the echo technique: Repeat a person's last few words as a question.

☑ For variety, throw in oh?, uh huh, hmmm, or nod your head.

☑ Don't ask questions that can be answered with a yes or no. Ask open-ended questions that require a thoughtful response.

☑ A lack of clear, complete communication is a major time-waster. It may take a little more time, but it will save far more time than it takes. In the words of an old paradox: Why is it that you never have time to do it right, but you always have time to do it over?

☑ Learn when to eliminate the "fat" from your conversations and get right to the "meat."

☑ Organize your conversations as you would a report: introduction, body, summary.

☑ Set aside time for occasional free-flowing, creative-thinking, brainstorming sessions.

☑ Don't wander off on tangents. Keep steering the conversation back on track.

☑ Ask for good feedback to make sure people understand you correctly. Give good feedback so others will know you understand them too.

☑ Make sure your body language is consistent with your verbal message.

☑ Restate your thoughts in several ways to help others understand better.

☑ Keep track of the details in your requests and conversations with others.

COMMUTING

Look for ways to use commuting time for something positive.

☑ Find out how much time you spend in transit. Analyze your travel time and what you do while traveling.

☑ Think about traveling at different times or using different routes to save time.

☑ Use commuting time to think and organize your thoughts.

☑ If possible, do job-related reading.

☑ Use commuting time to analyze problems or opportunities.

☑ Listen to cassette tapes. The average commute is about an hour each way, every day. Turn your car into a learning center.

☑ Consider the possibilities of moving closer to work. Or try to join the growing numbers of people who work at home and telecommute to the office.

☑ Consider working from your home. Computers and modems make this very easy for an increasing number of people.

☑ Consider altering the timing of your commute to take advantage of traffic patterns.

☑ Make telephone calls with your cellular phone.

☑ Have someone else do the driving so you can use the time more productively.

COMPUTER CLUTTER

Go through your computer directory regularly to delete unneeded files and programs.

☑ Junk accumulates on your hard drive at least as fast as it does on your desk. You need to clean out your hard drive at least as often as you clean out your regular filing cabinets.

☑ If you want to keep specific files but you don't use them very much, transfer the files to a floppy disk for safekeeping. Label it properly and file it. You don't need to make a hard copy of the documents. The new Zip drive is especially good for storing material or for backup.

☑ If you can't remember what the files are, it's a good idea to view them before you delete them.

☑ Sometimes you can decide whether or not to delete files simply by looking at the date they were created to see how old they are.

☑ At least once a year, review all the programs you have installed on your computer. Delete any that you aren't using any longer. This is a lot easier if you are using Windows 95, or if you use software designed to uninstall Windows programs, such as Uninstaller (MicroHelp, 800-922-3383).

☑ Archive old files on Zip disks or on tape back-up cartridges.

☑ If you're not sure whether you need to save a file on your computer, save it to a "maybe" disk. Files you refer back to can be transferred to the hard drive. After a few weeks or months go by, you can delete whatever is left on the "maybe" disk.

COMPUTERS

Make friends with your computer. It can be a huge time saver for you.

☑ Keep your Rolodex on your computer. You may even want to invest in a business card scanner, such as CardScan (Corex Technologies, 233 Harvard Street, Brookline, MA 02146; 800-942-6739). This program allows you to scan business cards quickly into word processing programs, such as WordPerfect, or into contact management programs, such as ACT!

☑ Consider using a computerized contact manager. These programs automatically move unfinished items to another day. A good one is ACT! Contact manager software helps you schedule appointments, track follow-up work, track joint projects with other people, keep detailed notes of conversations and meetings, and send letters, faxes, and proposals on time.

☑ Some people prefer to keep their to-do lists in the computer, while others say it's faster and easier to keep them on paper. In most cases, it's simply a matter of personal preference. The important thing is not whether you use the computer or paper for your planning, but whether you plan at all.

☑ Get different glasses for the computer. Reading glasses are made with a focal length of about 16 to 18 inches. You need a focal length of about 24 inches for the computer. Measure the distance from your eyes to the monitor when you're sitting at your desk.

☑ Get a good on-line service, such as CompuServe or America Online. You can take advantage of bulletin boards, databases, e-mail, technical questions on software, news stories, international weather information, plus access to the Internet.

☑ Like it or not, computers are here to stay. The greater your computer skills, the more you'll discover ways to save time with your computer.

☑ Don't expect the computer to be a panacea for everything. Wonderful as they may be, they won't do some things. For example, they won't make decisions for you or explain what you don't understand.

☑ Notebook computers can be a huge time saver. You can take them anywhere and work wherever you are. The newest batteries now provide over 6 hours operating time between recharges.

CRISES

Relax and think for a few minutes before tackling a crisis; don't just react.

☑ Most crises are the result of poor planning, poor coordination, or poor follow-up.

☑ Instead of immediately reacting, relax for a few minutes before you tackle a crisis, and prepare yourself to perform at your best.

☑ When a crisis does occur, think first. Maybe you can use the crisis as an opportunity to try something new.

☑ Keep records of your crises. Analyze them and look for patterns. Are they recurring crises or unique crises? Can any of your crises be predicted?

☑ If faced with constantly recurring crises, find out why things keep going wrong and fix them. Are they your fault or someone else's?

☑ Don't overreact to something that is not really a crisis. Don't invest more time and energy than a situation is worth.

☑ Set deadlines for yourself and others. Don't ignore them.

☑ Make sure your deadlines and time estimates are realistic.

☑ Meet regularly with subordinates, superiors, team members, and other key people to discuss and coordinate priorities and activities.

☑ Anticipate problems and consider contingency plans. Check regularly with others to help spot potential problems that may be brewing.

☑ Start early. Give people as much lead time as possible. The more people involved, the earlier you should start.

☑ Avoid unnecessary assumptions. Check things out.

☑ Review your progress often. Think about ways to improve performance.

☑ Improve your follow-up and feedback systems. Stay on top of the details.

☑ Be sure to follow up in a timely fashion. Make sure things happen when they should.

☑ Constantly improve your systems and procedures. Develop checklists and standard routines. Streamline everything you can.

☑ Improve your decision-making procedures. Get the facts, set goals, investigate alternatives and negative consequences, make the decision, and implement it.

☑ Take time to do it right the first time. You won't waste time doing it over.

☑ Turn a crisis into an opportunity to try new ideas, develop new procedures, and find better ways of doing things.

☑ You don't necessarily have to drop everything just because someone else has a problem. What if you weren't at work today? What would the person do? Why can't she or he try that even though you are here?

☑ Allow time for unforeseen problems that pop up every day.

☑ Give yourself as much time as necessary to think before responding or deciding. It's sometimes a good idea to "sleep on it" overnight before responding.

DELEGATION

**Delegate as often as you can ...
it gains time, increases motivation,
and builds people.**

☑ To perform well, people need to know (a) what they are expected to do; (b) how well they are expected to do it; (c) what resources they have to do it; and, (d) how well they did it.

☑ Fear blocks delegation. If you're reluctant to delegate, ask yourself: "What am I afraid of?" Learn to confront your fears positively.

☑ List everything you could delegate in your job. Decide to whom each item should be delegated. Delegate it.

☑ The person you should delegate a job to is not always the person you can most trust to get it done. Sometimes you need to delegate to the person who needs that assignment.

☑ Delegation failure is most often the fault of the delegator.

DELEGATION ANALYSIS

TASKS I MIGHT DELEGATE	WHO COULD I DELEGATE THEM TO?	TASKS I AM UNCERTAIN ABOUT DELEGATING	THINGS I CANNOT DELEGATE

☑ Don't delegate a job which should be discarded; eliminate it.

☑ There are seven steps for successful delegation: (1) Clarify all the intended results; (2) agree on the responsibility and authority level; (3) set checkpoints and controls; (4) provide adequate training; (5) create a motivating environment; (6) require completed work; (7) hold your people accountable for their performance.

☑ Consider the personality style of the other person. Adapt your delegation accordingly.

☑ Tell people what you expect. Make sure they understand. Tell them what priority you believe the job deserves. Discuss both importance and urgency.

☑ Don't confuse assigning work with delegating. Delegation involves the authority to act and make decisions.

☑ Give delegatees a deadline for completion, as well as intermediate deadlines, if appropriate. Insist on timely performance and reports.

☑ Consider how you will control the job before you delegate it. If you can't control it, don't delegate it.

☑ Don't interfere, undercut, overrule, or arbitrarily reverse subordinates' decisions.

☑ Delegate the right to be wrong. Use mistakes as a learning process.

☑ Be sure to delegate enough authority to enable the person to accomplish the intended results. There are eight levels of authority:

1. Get the facts, I'll decide.
2. Report the pros and cons of alternatives, I'll decide.
3. Recommend action, I'll decide.
4. Decide action, wait for my approval.
5. Decide action, act unless I say not to.
6. Act, tell me what happens.
7. Act, tell me only if it is unsuccessful.
8. Act, no reporting necessary.

☑ Write out the pertinent details of the delegation. Give the other person a copy.

☑ Follow-up does not mean breathing down a person's neck. Leave the person alone to do the job, but maintain regular checks at critical points along the way.

☑ Be available for questions, but don't hover. Leave the delegatee alone to do the work. Hovering hinders performance and signals a lack of trust.

☑ Be sure to check at agreed times. Missing checkpoints sends the wrong message.

☑ Don't allow upward delegation. Ask for solutions, not just problems. Help people learn to make good decisions, but don't make their decisions for them.

☑ Take time to create a motivating environment where people will be encouraged to seek and accept more responsibility.

☑ Insist on results, but not perfection. There are usually many ways to get the same result. Don't insist that other people do it your way. Learn to live with differences.

☑ Analyze your delegation patterns. Do you overdelegate to some and underdelegate to others? Are you reluctant to

DELEGATION PLANNER

PERSON	PROJECT	IMPORTANCE	HIGH	MED	LOW
		URGENCY	HIGH	MED	LOW

WHY THIS PERSON?	COMPLETION DEADLINE	DEGREE OF RISK	HIGH	MED	LOW
		RATE OF CHANGE	HIGH	MED	LOW

RESPONSIBILITY
RESULTS TO BE ACHIEVED • PERFORMANCE OBJECTIVES

....

....

....

....

....

....

....

....

AUTHORITY LEVEL INTENDED

1 = GET FACTS, I'LL DECIDE

2 = REPORT PROS & CONS, I'LL DECIDE

3 = RECOMMEND ACTION, I'LL DECIDE

4 = DECIDE ACTION, WAIT FOR MY APPROVAL

5 = DECIDE ACTION, ACT UNLESS I VETO

6 = ACT, TELL ME RESULTS

7 = ACT, TELL ME IF PROBLEM

8 = ACT, NO REPORT NEEDED

RESOURCES

....

....

....

....

....

....

....

ACCOUNTABILITY
CONTROLS • CHECKPOINTS • DUE DATES • HOW WILL PROGRESS BE MONITORED?

....

....

....

....

....

....

....

....

....

DELEGATION CHECKLIST
DID YOU...

MAKE SURE THE PROJECT ADDS VALUE?

GIVE CLEAR INSTRUCTIONS?

GIVE COMPLETE INFORMATION?

ENCOURAGE TWO-WAY CONVERSATION?

LISTEN CAREFULLY?

ENCOURAGE QUESTIONS?

MAKE NO ASSUMPTIONS?

DEFINE ALL TERMS?

SET APPROPRIATE CONTROLS?

GIVE ENOUGH AUTHORITY?

CLARIFY CHECKPOINTS?

CLARIFY REPORTING REQUIRED?

(continued)

FOLLOW-UP

DATE	COMMENTS—NOTES	DATE	COMMENTS—NOTES

delegate high levels of authority regardless of a subordinate's skill level? Do you have a plan for developing each of your subordinates so you can delegate more?

☑ When delegating, remember to ask; don't demand.

☑ Don't delegate tasks you aren't familiar with yourself.

☑ Pitch in and help when necessary.

☑ Give lots of praise and credit for a job well done.

☑ Be sure to check progress in time to take corrective action.

DESK

A desk is a tool to help you work efficiently.

☑ A stand-up desk may help you get more done in less time and feel less fatigued at the end of the day. Contact the Stand-Up Desk Company, 5207 Baltimore Avenue, Bethesda, MD 20816; 301-657-3630.

☑ If you don't need a desk, get rid of it. No desk, no clutter. Not having a desk forces you to rethink your entire job, and that's usually a good idea.

☑ If you don't really need desk drawers, consider using a table instead of a desk. No drawers, no clutter. People using tables rave about them. Tables are usually cheaper than desks, too.

☑ If you must have a desk, pick the right one. Remember, your desk is a tool, and it should help you work efficiently.

☑ When selecting a desk, make sure the top is large enough to accommodate all the equipment you need and still leave you plenty of space to work. Stay away from glass tops and highly polished surfaces which create glare. Dark tops contrasting with white paper also places extra strain on your eyes.

☑ Get as many pullouts as you can with your desk. Pullouts on the visitor's side are especially useful when visitors need a temporary work space.

☑ You should always be able to see the top of your desk. You can only work on one thing at a time. Put everything else away; that's what the drawers are for. Stuff all over your desk distracts you and makes it more difficult to concentrate on the job at hand.

☑ Buy the best chair you can afford. A top-of-the-line ergonomic chair will keep you relaxed and refreshed all day. A bad chair compounds fatigue and muscle problems. If you have a choice, economize on the desk and buy an excellent chair. If you spend a lot of time at your desk, the extra cost is a smart investment.

DETAILS

**The ability to stay on top of the details
separates winners from losers.
It's not the big things that get you;
it's the little ones.**

☑ Staying on top of the details involves a systematic way to identify the details, arrange the details, remember the details, and act on the details.

☑ Ask questions to help uncover all the critical pieces: What is the intended purpose of the project or job? What is the deadline? What relationships exist among the key parts? What are the key activities and milestones? Who will be responsible for each part? What is the deadline for each part? When must each part be started? What facilities, equipment, or materials are required for each activity?

☑ Ask two questions to help identify the proper sequence of activities: (1) What must come right before this step? (2) What must come right after this step?

PROJECT PLANNER—KEY ACTIVITIES

PROJECT NAME		DATE CREATED		DUE DATE	

PROJECT OBJECTIVES— INTENDED RESULTS

KEY PROJECT ACTIVITIES	TIME NEEDED	START DATE	DUE DATE	PERSON RESPONSIBLE	RESOURCES NEEDED

☑ To arrange activities logically, use the "sort and shuffle" technique. (1) Record activities on 3x5 cards, one activity on each card. (2) Spread the cards out on the table or floor. (3) Rearrange the cards in sensible groupings. (4) Review each activity and ask the two sequencing questions listed above.

☑ Develop a flowchart to help understand and explain your project. A flowchart is a good way to illustrate the relationships between all the parts.

☑ Programs such as Visio enable you to create Gantt charts quickly and easily.

☑ Make time to keep key people informed. Consider who needs to know, what they need to know, when they need to know it, and how you will tell them.

☑ If the same project is going to be done several times or by different people, make up a checklist for others to follow.

☑ Use tickler files to remind you when to start specific activities. You can do this manually or on your computer.

☑ Write down all the details that come your way through conversations, voice mail, telephone calls, electronic mail, or meetings.

DICTATION

Dictating machines increase your flexibility and options.

☑ Even in this age of computers, dictating machines are still a good idea for making notes, for capturing your thoughts while you're on the go, for issuing instructions to others, or even for exchanging information with visually impaired people.

☑ Dictating is 4 to 6 times faster than handwriting and about 2 to 3 times faster than the average person can keyboard.

☑ Anything that can be written can be dictated. It's only the preparation that differs. For example, to dictate numbers, you have to first decide on a standard format and tell the typist what it is. This same kind of thinking pattern is also useful in other instances, such as giving instructions to someone else.

☑ Take time to become familiar with the equipment. How does it feel? How does it operate? Read the instruction manual.

☑ Collect all the materials you'll need before you start. Make sure the equipment is working. Check the batteries.

☑ Outline your thoughts before you start. Why are you writing? What do you hope to achieve? What do you want the reader to think or do?

☑ Dictate all instructions to the typist first. Use a checklist to make sure you included everything.

☑ Speak distinctly. Remove everything from your mouth. Don't mumble. Speak in a conversational tone since it's easier to listen to.

☑ Spell out anything that may be confusing: names, sound-alike words, technical terms, addresses, problem words.

☑ Use standard form letters, paragraphs, phrases. Dictate by code.

☑ The Lanier VoiceWriter is a unique dictating machine that holds four tapes at once. This makes it much more versatile than an ordinary dictating machine. Lanier Voice Products, 1700 Chantilly Drive, Atlanta, GA 30324; 800-241-1706.

☑ If you plan to dictate in noisy conditions, test the equipment in actual situations before you buy it. Some machines will blank out background noise, and some won't.

DISTRACTIONS

Eliminate any distractions you can, and learn to ignore the rest.

☑ Study your work environment. The way furniture and equipment are arranged helps determine the number of interruptions and the noise level. Items like coffee pots and copy machines attract people.

☑ If you use modular office arrangements, be sure to provide quiet rooms for people who really need them.

☑ Place signs or lights at the front of large office areas to indicate whether or not people are actually in their work spaces. This discourages people from wandering around looking for others.

☑ Use white-noise machines to help blank out background noise. Even a small fan can help in a small area. Put sound-absorbing materials on the walls.

☑ Sucking on hard candy, or something similar, will help you concentrate on the job at hand.

☑ Wearing earphones makes it easier for you to focus on what you are doing without allowing distractions to bother you.

☑ Check out the Noisebuster made by Noise Cancellation Technologies, Inc., 800 Summer Street, Stamford, CT 06901; 800-278-3526. These innovative headphones actually cancel out background noise electronically.

☑ Force yourself to stick to the job at hand, even if it is boring. Train yourself to ignore nearby conversations. Don't allow any handy distraction to sidetrack your efforts.

☑ In open work areas, turn down the level of telephone bells or buzzers. Better still, turn the telephone ringers off, and use blinking lights instead.

☑ Carefully consider the flow of work and people when designing your office space. Poor designs increase the number of interruptions.

☑ To keep bright ideas or sudden thoughts from diverting you, jot down a quick note and get back to the task at hand.

DROP-INS

The best way to reduce drop-ins is by bunching things together and handling several items in one visit.

☑ If you bunch things together and handle several items in one visit, the items take only about 25 percent as much time to handle. You have fewer drop-ins, and you get more done in less time, too.

☑ Encourage people to set appointments instead of relying on unscheduled drop-in visits.

☑ Stand up when someone drops into your office. It is more polite, and you will automatically give them your full attention. The interruption will not last as long. It is also easier to get rid of them if they never get seated.

☑ Be candid with "gottaminits." Learn to say "no" when you should.

☑ Drop-ins are usually the people you work with. Encourage them to think things through for themselves...to do

INTERRUPTION RECORD

T = TELEPHONE CALL   **V = DROP-IN VISITOR**

T	V	WHO	PURPOSE—TOPICS DISCUSSED	BEG TIME	END TIME	TOTAL TIME

their homework before they bring the problem to you. Most people aren't really prepared to talk to you when they ask if you've "gottaminit."

☑ Don't contribute to small talk. Get right to the point and stay there.

☑ Go to the other person's office if she or he must see you. You will have more control of when to leave.

☑ Anticipate the information people want and provide it to them before they ask for it.

☑ To cut down on casual passerby interruptions, rearrange your furniture so you don't face the door or the traffic flow. If people can't see your eyes when they walk by, they won't stop to say hello.

☑ Reorganize your workflow or the timing of your tasks to minimize the problem of drop-ins.

☑ Don't drop in excessively on other people, especially your immediate staff.

☑ Keep track of all your drop-ins for a few days and look for patterns. You will see lots of possibilities for improvement.

EFFICIENCY

Most of us are more concerned with doing things right than with doing the right things.

- ☑ Peter Drucker wrote that, "Most people are more concerned with doing things right than with doing the right things." In other words, most of us are more concerned with being efficient than with being effective.

- ☑ Efficiency is doing things right; effectiveness is doing the right things. The best combination is to do the right things right.

- ☑ Efficiency is doing things faster, cheaper, using fewer people or materials, doing them in fewer steps.

- ☑ Effectiveness means accomplishing the goal, achieving the intended results.

- ☑ Concentrate first on effectiveness, then on efficiency. Ask yourself what needs to be done to achieve the intended results. Then ask what is the best way to do these activities.

☑ To increase productivity, Drucker suggests, "Give people something important to do and make sure they do it."

☑ There is no point in trying to do well what shouldn't be done at all. Drop work that doesn't contribute to goals. Evaluate work to see if it is still useful.

ELECTRONIC MAIL

**Electronic mail can be a
huge time saver; but be sure to
keep junk out of the system.**

☑ Try to limit your message to one screen. This makes it faster and easier for the receiver to read it.

☑ Use bullet statements to make your points stand out better.

☑ Be sure to state the purpose of your message clearly at the beginning.

☑ If you want a reply, say so at the beginning of your message.

☑ If you need a particular response, indicate exactly what you need and when you need it.

☑ Make it easy for the other person to respond. Whenever possible, offer check-off options, yes/no responses, or similar devices.

☑ Don't respond to e-mail messages if it is not necessary.

☑ When you do respond, keep your response as short as possible.

☑ Don't print out e-mail messages unless you really need hard copies.

☑ Be sure to describe any other documents you will be sending. If you must send a long message, attach it as a file transfer and write a brief description in the subject line.

☑ Set aside specific times to review your e-mail during the day. Don't let arrival of e-mail dictate your daily schedule. Don't let the arrival of e-mail interrupt important work unless the messages are really critical.

☑ Tell people you don't want to be copied on e-mail messages you don't really need.

☑ Keep in mind at all times that e-mail is not private. Other people can and do read your messages. Don't write anything you may regret later.

☑ Don't fill up the e-mail system with junk. Abuse has become so bad in some cases that companies are eliminating the entire e-mail system.

☑ Remember that there is no substitute for personal interaction. From time to time go see people face-to-face to maintain personal contacts.

ENERGY LEVEL

It takes a lot of energy to master time and perform at your best.

☑ Some of us are morning people, some are night people. Tackle important work when your energy level is highest. It's easier if this occurs early in the day.

☑ If your back hurts, get a new chair. A good ergonomic chair will enable you to work with less fatigue for much longer periods.

☑ Try thinking of the most pleasant or enjoyable thing you have to do today. It will motivate you to get moving.

☑ Keep a chart for a few weeks to determine where your energy level peaks throughout the day.

☑ Body heat varies as much as 3 degrees over the day. You are at your peak when your body temperature is at its peak. To raise your body heat, exercise in the morning. Once elevated, your temperature will stay high, lifting your entire day's cycle.

☑ Avoid energy robbers: inadequate sleep, poor nutrition, negative attitudes, drugs, alcohol.

☑ Rigorous exercise on a regular basis is a terrific energy generator. Exercising is one of the best ways to start the day.

FILING

**Paper is either worthwhile
or worthless; find a home for it
or throw it away.**

☑ Don't hold things in your office or on your desk simply because you don't know where to file it. It's either worthwhile or worthless. Find a home for it or throw it away.

☑ Realize that 95 percent of the things put in filing cabinets are never looked at again by anyone. Reconsider why you keep so much paper.

☑ Be sure to keep all active files handy so you won't have to go hunting for them. Active files should probably be kept within arm's reach of your desk.

☑ Use color coding to separate different kinds of files.

☑ Develop a system for keeping track of files which are removed. Much time is lost by trying to locate files that people have taken and forgotten to return. An easy solution is to use "File Out Cards." When people take a file, they note the file taken, the date, and their name on the card, and put the card where the file would have been.

☑ Don't clutter up file folders with trivia. Keep only useful information. Clean out the folder each time you use it.

☑ To determine what you need to file and what you can safely throw away, keep a record of what you actually use from your files for the next few months.

☑ To help decide whether to file something, ask questions. Is there a legal requirement for keeping this? How will I really use this within the next year? Do I really need it, or do I just want it? Can I get this information again if I ever need it? Does anyone else have a copy? What is the worst that can happen if I don't keep this?

☑ Establish a retention schedule and a destruct date for items placed in files. Be sure to clean out the files and throw things away on schedule.

☑ Keep your filing system simple. Use broad categories and plenty of file folders. Put like things together.

☑ Label everything. Choose names that match the way you think.

☑ It is often faster to handwrite the file labels. Printed labels are not always necessary.

☑ Keep most-often-used items closest to you. Consider using filing pockets that attach to the wall or hang over the partition.

☑ Consider using partitioned file folders. They help keep different items separated in the folder and easy to find.

☑ Have a file cleaning party once a year. Ask everyone to wear old clothes and go through every file drawer, every desk drawer, every shelf, and every closet. Throw out everything you don't need.

☑ Using expandable file pockets in file cabinet drawers is sometimes better than hanging folders. Experiment for yourself.

☑ Be consistent in putting information in the same place on each Rolodex card. Put the telephone number on top, since you use that most often. Attach business cards to the Rolodex card, or you might try scanning business cards into your computer with software such as CardScan.

☑ Attach a sheet to the outside of file drawers with a list of all files in the drawer. This makes it faster to find files you need without opening every drawer.

☑ If you can find things in less than 2 minutes, your system is working well; maybe you don't need to change it. Your system is your system. It doesn't have to look like anybody else's system.

FORMS

**Forms can be very useful
because they lead you through
a disciplined process of thinking.**

☑ Forms are more efficient. Standardize everything you can.

☑ Make sure all forms are well-designed and easy-to-use. A properly designed form is a huge time saver.

☑ Have parts of often-used forms preprinted to save time. For instance, preprint your name, address, and account number on expense reports. If you use FedEx or UPS, ask them to send preprinted air bills with your information and the addressee information preprinted on them.

☑ Samples of each form referred to in this book, plus many more, are available from the Time Management Center. You can order a master set of all our forms for making copies, or you can order all of them on diskette and easily reproduce any of our valuable forms on your word processor.

Time Management Center
1401 Johnson Ferry Road, Suite 328
Marietta, Georgia 30062
Telephone: 770-973-3977

GOALS

To stay focused on results, ask yourself: "Will what I'm doing right now help me achieve my goals?"

☑ Focus on results, not just on activities. It's not what you do that's so important, but what you get done.

☑ Clarify your long-range goals. Make sure you are aiming at something significant...what you really want.

☑ Don't try to keep your goals in your head; write out both personal goals and professional goals. Most of the people who write out their goals achieve them. Writing things down is a huge step forward.

☑ Be sure to set SMART goals: specific, measurable, achievable, relevant, and timed.

☑ Put up signs and pictures to remind you of your goals.

☑ Read your long-range goals at least once every day. This will make it easier to sort out all the trivia that comes your way. The more often you remind yourself what you're trying to achieve, the more likely you are to do the right things.

☑ Focus on your goals at all times. Constantly ask yourself, "Will what I am doing right now help me achieve my goals?" If the answer is no, then switch to something that will help.

☑ Never make a phone call, hold a meeting, or go see someone without first thinking about what you hope to achieve. When you stop thinking about intended results, you risk activity traps.

☑ Be sure you have at least one significant goal every day. Don't quit until you reach your daily goals. Before long, you will develop the habit of setting goals and reaching them.

☑ When conditions change, you may need to modify your goals. And, as you achieve your goals, be sure to set new ones.

☑ Set activity goals as well as results goals. Sometimes it is difficult to focus directly on results. Setting activity goals may help focus indirectly on results.

HABITS

**Pick your habits carefully.
When you choose a habit, you also
choose the results of that habit.**

☑ Habits control behavior. A habit is simply a behavior done so often that it becomes normal, natural, comfortable, and automatic.

☑ Most work-related habits can be changed within 3 to 4 weeks.

☑ Keep the good habits; replace the bad ones. A habit is good if it helps you achieve your goal; it is bad if it hinders your achievement.

☑ Earl Nightingale said, "Successful people form the habit of doing what failures don't like to do. They like the results they get by doing what they don't necessarily enjoy doing. Failures, though, will accept whatever results are possible by doing only what they like to do."

☑ Pogo: "We have met the enemy, and they is us."

☑ The ancient Greeks wrote, "It is not enough to know; you must also act. Knowledge without action is impotent." Good results require more than just good intentions.

☑ Old proverb: The more you do of what you're doing, the more you'll get of what you're getting.

☑ To become a better time manager, you must break out of your comfort zone.

☑ Most of us only change when we are forced to do so. However, you don't have to wait for external force; you can also use internal force.

☑ The key to willpower is "want-power." If you want something strongly enough, you will find the discipline necessary to do it.

☑ Self-discipline is easier if you stop thinking about it and simply do it.

☑ To create new habits: (1) describe the old habit you want to replace; (2) define the new habit; (3) begin as strongly as you can and tell others what you are doing; (4) never deviate from the new behavior; (5) use every opportunity to practice the new behavior; (6) consciously follow the new behavior until it becomes the dominate pattern; (7) ask others to help you change.

HOME

**The ideas that help you
master time at work will also
help you master time at home.**

☑ Keep a pad of paper by your bed. You never know when you'll wake up with a terrific idea.

☑ Having two wash basins in the bathroom speeds up the morning routine.

☑ Taking a shower requires less time than taking a bath.

☑ Organize your closet by categories so you can find things faster.

☑ Limit your wardrobe and you won't spend so much time deciding what to wear.

☑ Always wear the same accessories with each suit or dress. This will cut down on those little, agonizing decisions.

☑ Keep extra supplies of essential items.

☑ Use bulletin boards or white boards to turn any empty wall into a family communications center. A variety of different message boards can be purchased from Remarkable Products, 245 Pegasus Avenue, Northvale, NJ 07647-9941; 201-784-9000.

☑ Use rubber stamps or gummed labels with your name and address on them so you don't have to write it out all the time. X-Stamper makes excellent fold-up stamps you can easily carry with you. X-Stamper pads are available at most office supply stores.

☑ To speed up bill-paying chores, address a bunch of envelopes ahead of time. If you have a copier, you can address one envelope and run the others through the copier.

☑ Buy in large quantities and you'll have to shop less often.

☑ Analyze things you and your family have to do. Look for ways to simplify them or speed them up.

☑ Set goals and priorities for allocating home time.

☑ Eliminate jobs around the home that really don't need to be done. Farm out everything you can afford, like cleaning and lawn care.

☑ Use planning and scheduling techniques at home just as you would at work.

☑ Each family must set its own standard for what is considered important and what is considered to be a waste of time.

☑ Assign chores. There will be less arguing, and things will get done faster.

☑ Rotate tasks among family members.

☑ Keep lots of extras for those things that are easily lost or misplaced: umbrellas, pens, scissors, nail clippers, tissues, hangers, etc.

☑ Establish a place for everything, and do your best to keep everything where it belongs.

☑ Every time you buy something new, get rid of something old.

☑ Keep family records up-to-date. Make sure your surviving spouse or family can find all the information needed.

HURRY

**Slow down, you're going too fast...
got to make the morning last.**

☑ Dr. Larry Dossey: "Just as Pavlov's dogs learned to salivate inappropriately, we have learned to hurry inappropriately. Our sense of urgency is set off not by a real need to act quickly, but through learned cues. Our 'bells' have become the watch, the alarm clock, the morning coffee, and the hundreds of self-inflicted expectations that we build into our daily routine. The subliminal message from the watch and the clock is: time is running out; life is winding down; please hurry."

☑ Old proverb: "The hurrier I do, the behinder I get."

☑ Watch carefully to avoid "hurrysickness." Competition grows keener, the pace grows faster, technology becomes increasingly complex, information inundates us, and on all sides we are urged to hurry, hurry, hurry... go, go, go. To counter all this "hurryitis," learn to piddle and putter around with nothing much. Take time off, go for a drive, daydream, linger at dinner, go to a movie with a friend, take a nap in the hammock. Break away from the treadmill regularly.

☑ Slow down and take the time to put more quality back into your life. Learn to loaf a little. Remember, the time you enjoy wasting may not be a waste of time.

☑ Assess yourself. Hurrysickness shows up when you rush to be first at everything...when you continually press forward, even though you're not really getting anywhere...when you get mad if someone cuts in front of you even though the freeway is stalled with bumper-to-bumper traffic...when you finish someone else's sentences...when you drum your fingers impatiently...when you skip meals to save time...when you schedule children so heavily they hardly have time to breathe.

☑ Another help for hurryitis is to practice slowing down. Drive slower, walk slower, talk slower, eat slower, think slower.

IMPROVING

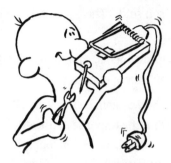

There is always a better way to do anything, but it's up to you to find it.

☑ Strive for continual improvement. Try to improve your job in some way every week. That's at least 50 improvements every year.

☑ Eliminate unnecessary activities.

☑ Stop doing things the hard way; look for easier, faster ways.

☑ Try to do two or three things at once.

☑ Regularly examine work procedures for jobs you are doing. What are the steps involved? Who does them? When are they done? Can any steps be eliminated or combined? Simplify everything you can.

☑ Ask your staff to help brainstorm for new ideas. Look for ways to eliminate steps, combine operations, shorten procedures, streamline paperwork, remove bottlenecks.

☑ If a procedure is repeated frequently, even slight improvements can create substantial productivity gains.

☑ Thomas Edison said, "There is always a better way to do anything."

☑ To find improvements, question everything, assume nothing, keep asking questions.

☑ Use Toyota's 5-W System: Why? Why? Why? Why? Why? No matter what the response is, ask why? By the time you get to the 5th level, you're probably dealing with root causes or foundational issues.

☑ Draw up a personal action plan to help you master your time, and get started.

☑ Get a group action plan started. Ask what can be done at your organization to help everyone use time better and be more productive. Do whatever you can. At least put your case to the people who can decide.

INDECISION

There is a time to deliberate...and a time to act. Learn to recognize which is which, and act accordingly.

☑ Make decisions when further information will probably add very little to the quality of the decision.

☑ Make a sincere effort to get the best information possible within the time available.

☑ Don't delay in a futile attempt to achieve perfection. Learn to take reasonable risks.

☑ Make a list of the advantages and disadvantages.

☑ Stop reciting all the "shoulds" that occur to you. Most of them are only self-imposed, artificial standards. Allow yourself to be a little less than perfect. Break the "rules" from time to time.

☑ Stop worrying that something will go wrong. Keep a worry list. Write down all the things you think will go wrong. Review the list from time to time to see how many of the things you worried about actually happened.

☑ Worrying is a waste of good work time. Don't worry about one project while you're working on another one.

☑ Worrying is also a waste of good play time. Don't think about work while you're trying to relax. Force your mind onto something so engrossing that you forget all about work. Don't take work on vacation. Don't worry about the kids while you're out for the evening.

INFORMATION

The information age requires new ways to collect information, process information, and store information.

☑ Linda Lederman, author of *Communications in the Workplace*: "In one year, the average American will read or complete 3000 notices and forms; scan 100 newspapers and 36 magazines; watch 2463 hours of television; listen to 730 hours of radio; buy 20 records; talk on the telephone almost 61 hours; read three books and spend countless hours exchanging information in conversation. Thus, we spend most of our waking hours with information."

☑ Spend some time with a reference librarian and learn about the various kinds of information resources available.

☑ Quincy Munford, Librarian of Congress: "Probably 95 out of 100 people never take advantage of shortcuts learned by others' experience because they don't know the information they need, and could put to use, is available, or where to get it quickly and effectively."

☑ There are three types of databases currently in use: one simply locates articles for you; the second offers summaries of material; and the third produces complete texts to read on-screen or download to print. Know which ones are best for your uses.

☑ Watch out for information anxiety, which is the gap between what we understand and what we think we should understand. No one can know everything they'd like to know. Concentrate on what is most important.

☑ To help decide what information you need, ask questions: Do I actually read all the magazines I receive? What information do I really have to keep up with? What information do I get too much of now? What information do I not get enough of now? What's the easiest way to get information? What are the most effective information sources? How can the computer help me?

INTERRUPTIONS

The best thing to do when facing lots of interruptions is to keep a record of them and look for patterns.

☑ Interruptions are part of your job. It may be your attitude that needs adjusting. Interruptions are more manageable when you have a positive attitude.

☑ William Ward: "Interruptions can be viewed as sources of irritation or opportunities for service, as moments lost or experience gained, as time wasted or horizons widened. They can annoy us or enrich us, get under our skin or give us a shot in the arm, monopolize our minutes or spice our schedules, depending on our attitude toward them."

☑ Interruptions have two basic causes: internal and external. The internal ones are the interruptions you cause yourself. Start fixing those first.

☑ After an interruption, train yourself to go right back to the task you were doing. Don't use the interruption as an excuse to drift aimlessly.

☑ Allow enough time for interruptions and other unscheduled events in your daily schedule. Most people need to allow at least 25 percent of the day for unexpected things. If you allow for them, you will be less frustrated when they do occur.

☑ Consider alternatives, such as electronic mail, voice mail, or fax. Even first class mail is becoming more popular again.

☑ Reorganize your work flow or the timing of your tasks to minimize interruptions or take advantage of naturally occurring quiet time. For example, you might work during the normal lunch hour and take your lunch early or late.

☑ Keep a record of all your interruptions. Find out who interrupts you, when it happens, how long it lasts, what it was about. Look for patterns. Records will help you define your specific interruption problems.

☑ Ask questions to help analyze your interruption log: What patterns do you see? How much time is involved in each pattern? Who or what caused the most interruptions? Do telephone calls take more or less time than visitors? How long did the interruption last? What are the longest uninterrupted periods? Is the morning different from the afternoon? What interruptions are not shown that you would expect to see? How many interruptions were important? How many were urgent? What suggestions could you offer to help improve this condition?

☑ Keep interruptions short and you will solve much of the problem.

INTERRUPTION RECORD

T = TELEPHONE CALL   **V = DROP-IN VISITOR**

T	V	WHO	PURPOSE—TOPICS DISCUSSED	BEG TIME	END TIME	TOTAL TIME

☑ Don't use the arrival of the daily mail, e-mail, or voice mail messages as an excuse for interrupting yourself. Learn to stay focused on the task at hand if it's an important one.

☑ Be careful that you don't subconsciously interrupt yourself just because you are bored, or procrastinating something you don't want to do.

☑ Tom Peters: "Pursue mindless interruptions. Allow for (plan for!) unplanned interruptions. I often find more useful information about 'life' in Section D of *USA Today* than in *The Wall Street Journal*. Most 'ahas,' mundane or grand, come from the juxtaposition of surprising streams of information."

JOB ANALYSIS

At least once a year, analyze your entire job: Consider what you *think* you're doing, what you *should be* doing, and what you are *actually* doing.

☑ At least once a year, analyze your entire job. What do you do? How important are the parts? How much time do you spend on the different parts? How much time should you be spending on the different parts?

☑ Ask your immediate superior to analyze your job and compare your analysis with your superior's analysis. Realize that superiors and subordinates seldom have the same perceptions. Differences are simply agendas for dialogue.

☑ Consider what you should be doing that you are not doing. How can you add something to your job? What would you have to take out?

☑ If it looks like much of your time is spent on trivial issues, consider what you can do instead that would make a better contribution. Try to rearrange your job.

KILLING TIME

**Time is life.
To waste your time
is to waste your life.**

☑ Benjamin Franklin said, "Dost thou love life? Then do not waste time, for that's the stuff life is made of."

☑ According to the Nielsen Report, the average American adult watches 49 hours of television every week. That's probably a huge waste of time.

☑ Think carefully about how you live your life. Most of us wind up with regrets about what we didn't do: not studying more, not taking more risks, not being more assertive, not spending quality time with our families. Live so you'll have few regrets.

☑ The difference between success and failure is about two hours a day. Use those two hours well and you'll forge ahead. Waste those two hours and you'll inevitably fall behind.

LISTS

A daily to-do list can be very useful— so can a not-to-do list.

☑ A daily to-do list is the most common planning tool in America. If you're not writing one out, you probably should be.

☑ In addition to a to-do list, make a not-to-do list. This is a list of things you should leave undone: anything you can delegate, things other people should be doing, low-priority tasks, things no one will notice if they're not done, anything you said "yes" to when you should have said "no."

☑ Make sure your daily to-do list has time estimates for each activity. Remember, you run out of time, not work.

☑ Most people say it's better to plan tomorrow before you leave work today, while things are fresher in your mind. It's also a good way to clear your mind and prepare for the evening.

☑ Be prepared for a productive start tomorrow morning. Set things out tonight before you leave so they'll be ready when you get back in.

☑ If you prepare your daily list the evening before, you are less likely to react to events in your day.

☑ Put priorities on your daily list, and start with the most important items first. Most people don't do this.

☑ Don't put more on your daily list than you can expect to get done. If you do, it's demotivating and a constant reminder of how much you're not getting done.

☑ If you don't finish some tasks on today's list, don't just automatically move them to the top of tomorrow's list. Think about their value and when they should be done.

MAIL

Use the DRAFT system to sort your incoming mail items.

☑ The DRAFT system sorts your incoming mail items into five groupings. D = items that must be distributed or delegated. R = items you must read. A = items you must act on. F = items you must file. T = items which can be thrown out.

☑ Mail is more than what comes from the post office. It also includes e-mail, voice mail, faxes, interoffice mail, FedEx, UPS, and similar sources. These are all sources of "paper" work requiring decisions.

☑ Eighty percent of your mail can probably be answered immediately when read. Don't set it aside. Do it now.

☑ Open your mail later in the day. You are less likely to react to it or allow it to set the tone for the day.

☑ Make marginal notations on letters and memos and send them along. Make copies only if you really need them.

☑ Try to throw out as much as you can without opening it. This is especially easy for post office mail. Don't waste time opening junk mail just out of curiosity.

☑ There are clues all over the envelope to help you decide what to toss and what to open: return address, postage rate, how stamped, color of envelope, type of envelope, size of envelope, how addressed, who addressed to, messages printed on envelope.

☑ Stand up to open your mail and you'll throw more away. Work off the top of a table or file cabinet with a wastebasket handy. Things that just need filing can also be quickly filed.

☑ Never put things back in the envelope after you've taken them out.

MASTER LIST

Keep a master list of all the things you need to take care of.

☑ Use a master to-do list. This is a running list of everything you have to do...all your unfinished work and ongoing projects. Use as many sheets of paper as necessary, or keep your list in the computer. Draw a line completely through an item when it is finished. Add new items to the bottom of the list. Don't make separate notes on anything else except your master to-do list. This provides one standard way to handle everything.

☑ If it concerns you, write it on your master list. For most people, this will be a record of all they have to do over the next several weeks. Put a due date by each item and an estimate of how much time will be needed for each item.

☑ Periodically compare items on your master list to your longer-range goals. Make sure that what you intend to tackle will help you toward your goals. If not, remove it from the master list.

MASTER TO-DO LIST

#	ACTIVITY	PRIORITY DESCRIPTION	DUE DATE	TIME NEEDED	START DATE

☑ When you make out your daily to-do list, check your master list to see what needs to be done tomorrow.

☑ Never put a piece of unfinished work inside a file folder without first noting it on your master list.

☑ Create a master file to hold the backup material for items on your master list.

MEETINGS (Before)

Good meetings do not just happen automatically. They must be carefully planned...

☑ Clarify the specific purpose of the meeting and be sure it is really necessary.

☑ Discontinue unnecessary meetings. Many meetings involve only one-way communication which does not require a meeting.

☑ Call a meeting to: clarify goals, receive verbal reports, get group discussion of ideas, analyze or solve problems, achieve acceptance, train or teach, reconcile conflict, discuss information, get immediate reactions, make sure the group understands your message, get feedback, get a group decision or consensus, assure uniform presentation of information, fulfill legal requirements.

☑ Consider the consequences of not having a meeting. Do not call a meeting when: other alternatives will work just as well, there is not enough time to prepare, key people are not available, timing is not right, speed is of primary importance, it will probably not produce desired results, it is more important to respond to individual needs, costs outweigh benefits.

☑ Consider alternatives to meetings, such as memos, conference calls, voice mail, electronic mail, or fax machines.

☑ Make decisions without meetings. Never use a committee or group if it can be done individually.

☑ Anticipate the people and information needed and be sure they're on hand.

☑ Invite only those people whose attendance is necessary. Tell them what you expect of them at the meeting.

☑ To prepare a good agenda: Consider the logical sequence of items so the agenda moves logically from point to point; be sure to identify what is being discussed, why it is being discussed, and what should be achieved by the discussion.

☑ Set time limits for each agenda item. Make sure the more important issues get the most time.

☑ Send the agenda out ahead of time and tell people what you expect from them.

☑ Keep the meeting small. You won't accomplish much with more than 5 to 8 people there. Invite only those who can make a contribution.

☑ Be prepared for the meeting yourself. Do your homework before arriving.

☑ If you think a meeting will be a waste of your time, don't go. If you must go, make sure the meeting won't be a waste of your time.

☑ If the time is not convenient for you, ask that the meeting be rescheduled.

☑ Confirm all meetings before you leave.

☑ Things to take with you to a meeting: pen or pencil, pad, calendar, schedule, business cards.

☑ Be specific about where the meeting will be held and how to get there.

☑ When people want an impromptu meeting, ask why they want to get together with you. Suggest alternatives.

☑ Distribute information before the meeting so people can be prepared to contribute when they get there.

MEETINGS (During)

Good meetings do not just happen automatically. They must be carefully planned, skillfully executed....

☑ Use an agenda and stick to it. Resist tangents. You can't control a meeting without a good agenda, and the agenda won't help if you ignore it.

☑ Set a time limit for your meeting. Start and stop on time.

☑ The best way to get people to a meeting on time is to always start on time.

☑ If minutes are required, have someone there just to take notes. You can't participate if you're taking notes.

☑ Use visual aids to clarify discussions. Pictures are often faster and easier to understand than words.

☑ Summarize the results of the meeting. Clarify or review all assignments.

☑ Hold stand-up meetings and you'll get more done in less time. You can even buy stand-up conference tables from the Stand-Up Desk Company, 5207 Baltimore Avenue, Bethesda, MD 20816; 301-657- 3630.

☑ Minimize small talk and side conversations. Don't contribute to these conversations yourself.

☑ Almost all impromptu meetings can be scheduled for later in the day, or even the next day, without any problems.

☑ Conference and meeting rooms shouldn't be too comfortable.

☑ Make sure there is a clock in the meeting room.

☑ To encourage promptness, ask the last person who arrives to take the minutes.

☑ Ask participants to stand when it's their turn to speak.

☑ Ask: "How will we know when this meeting is over?" This will help focus on closure for the meeting.

☑ Close and lock the door when it's time to start the meeting.

☑ Don't allow interruptions unless they are truly emergencies. Use the 100-mile rule: Would you call this person back to the office if they were 100 miles away? If you wouldn't, then don't interrupt them during the meeting.

☑ Breakfast meetings are usually faster than luncheon meetings.

☑ Coffee meetings are usually more productive and quicker than luncheon meetings.

☑ Structure discussion in stages: (a) State the proposition, (b) produce the evidence, (c) discuss what the evidence means, (d) reach a conclusion, (e) decide on the action.

☑ Stop people from jumping ahead or going back over old ground.

☑ Make action notes as you go along.

☑ Summarize all decisions and conclusions.

☑ Spend a few minutes at the end to critique the quality of your meeting; find out what you do well and what you could improve. Discuss ways to improve your meetings.

☑ To quickly find out what you need to improve about your meetings, ask everyone attending your meetings to anonymously answer a few questions. Was the meeting necessary? Was the purpose clear? Was the purpose achieved? Did the meeting start and stop on time? Was an agenda used? Did discussion stick to the subject? Were interruptions blocked? Were the right people there? Were they prepared? Did they participate effectively? Was the meeting well organized? Were assignments clear? Was the meeting worth what it cost?

MEETINGS (After)

Good meetings do not just happen automatically. They must be carefully planned, skillfully executed, and diligently followed up.

☑ Prepare a follow-up action plan. Note what must be done, who will do it, when it is due. Give a copy to everyone at the end of the meeting.

☑ Make sure people know what actions they are responsible for after the meeting ends and when the assignments are due.

☑ If minutes are necessary, distribute them within 24 hours.

☑ Be sure to check the progress of action assignments. Don't risk finding out at the next meeting that nothing has happened.

MEMORY

Writing things down is usually better than trying to remember them.

☑ Your memory works easier when your thoughts are well organized.

☑ To improve your memory: concentrate on remembering, break out of your routine, picture what you want to remember, and try using mnemonic devices.

☑ Be aware of factors affecting your memory: amount of rest, medications, alcohol, sickness, hay fever, colds, etc.

☑ Learn to trust your memory. Tell yourself you have a good memory. If you keep saying you have a poor memory, then you will have a poor memory.

☑ Intend to remember. Pay attention. Ask questions. Make mental notes.

☑ Exercise your memory. The "use it or lose it" principle definitely applies here.

☑ Make sure you understand what you want to remember. Comprehension is a key factor to remembering because it helps your brain connect thoughts in "semantic networks" of meaning.

☑ Decide what things you don't need to remember.

☑ The key to memory is association and repetition.

MORNING ROUTINE

**For a good, productive day,
get an early start.**

☑ Before you go to bed, do anything you can to simplify the morning rush. For example, you can decide what to wear tomorrow and lay out the clothes you want in advance.

☑ Get up when you wake up. Laying in bed when you can't sleep will make you tired and groggy.

☑ Rearrange items in your bathroom so the most frequently used items are in front and easily accessible.

☑ Taking a shower is faster than taking a bath.

☑ Always wear the same accessories with each suit, or dress to minimize decision making in the morning.

☑ When you start thinking about the day ahead of you, try thinking about the most enjoyable or most rewarding things you have to do.

☑ Make up individual breakfast trays for each family member the evening before. The trays can go to and return from wherever each person wants to eat in one trip.

☑ Try working at your bed when you wake up. Make sure you have everything you need to actually work in bed.

☑ Try a prebreakfast work segment. Use breakfast as a reward for getting something done. You can go to the office, or you can work right at your bed.

☑ Get an early start. This might mean starting at an earlier hour, starting to work when you get to work, or starting on projects earlier.

☑ Get a productive start. Be sure your first hour at work is productive. The way you start the day sets a pattern for the entire day.

☑ Be prepared for a productive start tomorrow morning. Set things out tonight before you leave so they'll be ready and waiting for you when you arrive tomorrow.

☑ To function at your best in the morning, get plenty of sleep, exercise regularly, and eat a nutritional breakfast.

MYTHS

Something isn't working right...

Be careful about making assumptions; they may not be true.

- ☑ Most people are overworked, owing to the nature of their jobs. (False)

- ☑ Your job is unique and not subject to repetitive time patterns. (False)

- ☑ People at higher levels make better decisions. (False)

- ☑ Your job deals with serving people, and since all people are important, you can't establish priorities. (False)

- ☑ Most people can solve their time problems by working harder. (False)

- ☑ Efficiency and effectiveness are essentially the same thing. (False)

- ☑ Most of the ordinary daily activities don't need to be planned. (False)

- ☑ It isn't possible to always work on the basis of priorities. (False)

- ☑ Most people know how they spend their time. (False)

- ☑ Busy, active people get the best results. (False)

- ☑ Managing time doesn't allow for spontaneous actions. (False)

- ☑ It isn't necessary to write out your goals. (False)

- ☑ You do your best work under the pressure of a deadline. (False)

- ☑ An open-door policy improves effectiveness in dealing with others. (False)

- ☑ Quiet time just won't work in most offices. (False)

- ☑ It's better to do the quick, easy tasks first so you'll have more time for the big ones later. (False)

- ☑ The more urgent something is, the more important it is. (False)

NOTEBOOK PLANNERS

Notebook planners can help you organize your work and your time.

☑ Use a good notebook planner system. About 70 percent of the people in business now use them. It doesn't matter which one you buy, since they're all pretty much the same. However, some may have features that will be more useful for you than others.

☑ Most notebook planners are also available in computerized versions. And some of the contact management programs will also print out pages that are compatible with several of the best-selling notebook planners.

☑ There are eight common elements of a good notebook planner: (1) a yearly calendar, (2) a monthly calendar to make notes on, (3) planning sheets for each day, (4) telephone and address pages, (5) a set of A-Z tabs, (6) sets of other tabs with labels you can customize, (7) a variety of specialized pages, (8) a sheet for keeping track of notes and discussions with others.

☑ For best results, select one which has a spot for estimating task time on the planning page. This is a key part of planning your time, yet many notebooks omit it.

☑ Make sure you can customize your notebook any way you like. The ones with more than three rings are difficult to customize.

☑ Size is also a matter of personal preference. About 30 percent of the people using notebooks carry the $8^1/2$ x 11 version; about 50 percent carry the $5^1/2$ x $8^1/2$ version; and about 20 percent carry pocket-size versions.

☑ Use the A-Z tabs to file backup material for action items noted on the daily pages. This is like having a cross-indexed tickler file inside your notebook. Everything you need is always with you. You can keep about 100 extra sheets of paper in most notebooks.

☑ Label tabs for people you interact with constantly. Keep notes of your conversations and things you want to talk with them about. You won't forget, and you'll interrupt them less.

☑ Here's how to get information on several of the most popular notebook planning systems:

Day Runner, Inc.
3562 Eastham Drive
Culver City, CA 90232
800-635-5544

Day-Timer, Inc.
One Day-Timer Plaza
Allentown, PA 18195
800-225-5005

Executive ScanCard Systems
814 West Third Avenue
Columbus, OH 43212
800-848-2618

Franklin Quest, Inc.
2640 Decker Lake Boulevard
Salt Lake City, UT 84125
800-654-1776

Time Design
Suite 450
11835 West Olympic Boulevard
Los Angeles, CA 90064
800-637-9942

Time Resources, Inc.
239 Littleton Road, Suite 8-A
Westford, MA 01886
800-358-8463

NOTES

How do you spell xpukdht?

Develop the habit of making good notes when you talk with people.

☑ Stop using small slips of paper to make notes. They're easily lost and hard to keep track of. Instead, use regular $8^1/_2$ x 11 sheets of paper. Tape small slips to full-size sheets, or make copies on full-size sheets.

☑ Get in the habit of taking good notes when you talk with people on the telephone, in meetings, or wherever you are. When you're finished with the conversation, be sure to file your notes in the proper file folder or in your tickler system.

☑ The ordinary call return slips are too small and easily lost on your desk. Instead, make call return slips on $8^1/_2$ x 11 sheets so they'll stand out. They also have plenty of room for making notes during the call. You might even want to color-code them.

☑ Post-it® Notes can be used for anything: to remind your-self of things, to mark places in a book, to make notes on magazine pages, to stick notes on someone's computer monitor, to indicate actions, to indicate corrections, etc. There must be at least a million uses for Post-it® Notes. And they come in any size you want.

☑ When you note someone's name and address, be sure to get all their various numbers: telephone, fax, e-mail, Internet. Also, ask for the best time to call them.

OPEN-DOOR POLICY

**An open door means you are accessible
but not necessarily instantly available
for any spontaneous drop-in
that wanders by.**

☑ An open-door policy doesn't mean that you must be literally at the beck and call of anyone who shows up at your door...always ready at their convenience. The philosophy underlying the open-door policy is that you should be easily accessible to those who really need you. There should not be any unnecessary barriers between you and them. This philosophy can be easily implemented even if your office door is physically closed.

☑ Rethink your open-door policy. Many of them have deteriorated to an "always available" policy. Whoever walks through the door at any time controls your day.

☑ Redefine your open-door policy so that "open" means accessible. You can be accessible even though your door is closed. However, the closed door will discourage trivial and unimportant interruptions.

☑ Don't hesitate to say, "I'm tied up at the moment; can we get together later?"

☑ Schedule regular times to meet with staff, colleagues, peers, and superiors. Be diligent in keeping these appointments.

ORGANIZING

Too much work, too little time.

Things, tasks, and time all need to be better organized.

☑ Getting organized involves three issues: things, tasks, and time. Organizing things makes you neater. Organizing tasks and time make you more productive.

☑ At the end of the day or the end of the week, spend a few minutes to get organized. File anything that should have been filed. Add items to your master list, tickler files, or notebook planner. Put stuff away and leave with a clean desk behind you.

☑ Develop the habit of going through all the things that accumulate on your desk during the day before you go home. You'll find it's much easier to stay organized.

☑ Organizing tasks and time involves clarifying goals, determining priorities, and planning and scheduling activities. See the sections on Planning and Scheduling for more tips.

PAPERWORK

There are only four things you can do with paper: dump it, delegate it, do it, or delay it.

☑ Never set aside a piece of action paper until you have taken some action, or at least scheduled the first step.

☑ Keep your desktop cleared for action. Get rid of clutter. Put all the paper where it belongs.

☑ You can only work on one thing at a time. Everything else should be put away in its proper place, easily retrievable when you need it. You will concentrate better when you have only one thing demanding your attention.

☑ To get control of your paper, ask three questions: (1) Will I really do anything with it? (2) When will I do it? (3) Where will I keep it?

☑ Get a "maybe" box. Work on important paper, throw away junk paper, put everything else in the "maybe" box. If you ever need it, you'll know where it is. When the box gets full, dump it.

☑ Use tickler files to help keep track of the details and maintain timely follow-up.

☑ To cut the flow to your in-basket: Don't record it. Don't ask for it. Throw it away. Discontinue it. Question its purpose.

☑ Develop criteria for what to keep and what to throw out. Don't keep it if it won't be useful.

☑ Don't let people dump mail randomly on your desk. Arrange a place for incoming mail that's out of the way.

☑ Open your mail later in the day. If you open the mail early in the day, you're more likely to react to it and waste time with trivial mail.

☑ Develop routines and standard responses, streamline everything you can. Simplify all reports.

☑ Use computers, dictating machines, electronic mail, voice mail, and fax to help speed up your paperwork chores.

☑ Schedule regular work sessions for your paperwork. Try setting aside specific times of day for particular kinds of paperwork.

☑ Make notes in the margin, and send it along.

☑ If possible, handle each piece of paper only once. Do whatever needs to be done the first time you pick it up. Don't set it aside without taking some action on it. This will keep it from getting lost or forgotten about.

☑ Consider using a stand-up desk or table. It's often a faster and less fatiguing way to work. Contact the Stand-Up Desk Company, 5207 Baltimore Avenue, Bethesda, MD 20816; 301-657-3630.

☑ Most people spend too much time on their paperwork. Set time limits. Try to finish within the time allowed. Keep cutting the time down. Force yourself to find quicker ways to handle things.

☑ Clean out your files at least once a year. Have a party doing it!

☑ Analyze your paperwork to see what can be eliminated, shortened, modified, combined, or otherwise improved.

☑ Stop procrastinating. Your paperwork won't go away by itself.

☑ Date all papers and notes.

☑ When in doubt, throw it out.

☑ Develop routines around paperwork. Set aside a certain time and a certain place for doing particular kinds of paperwork.

☑ Do your best to resist paper. Most of us are actually drawn to paper and treat it like some kind of security blanket. Experts estimate we could throw out at least 40 to 50 percent of our paper and never miss it.

☑ Provide incentives for people who discover ways to trim the paperwork problem in your company.

☑ Periodically analyze all paperwork generated in your company. Try to eliminate as much as you can. Modify and simplify the rest to reduce the time people spend on it.

☑ Set aside a specific time during the day for handling different kinds of paperwork. This will help you develop routine paperwork-handling habits.

☑ Use the 10-percent rule. You'll usually find that you can do an adequate job in about 10 percent of the time it takes to do a "perfect" job. This doesn't mean sloppy workmanship, but an appropriate response.

☑ Ask for verbal reports instead of written ones whenever possible. People prefer to do it this way, too.

☑ Get a smaller briefcase. You won't be able to take so much paper home at night.

☑ Reduce the number of copies you distribute to a bare minimum. Require that people justify why they should receive, or continue to receive, every report that goes to them.

☑ To get people to respond rapidly to your memos and reports, try clipping a short note to the top which explains why it is to their benefit to read and act on your material quickly.

☑ Look for ideas, tools, and techniques that will help you streamline your paperwork. Notice how other people and offices handle their paper. Browse through large office-products catalogs or visit a well-stocked office supply store.

PERFECTIONISM

Learn to recognize the difference between striving for excellence and striving for perfection.

☑ Learn to recognize the difference between striving for excellence and striving for perfection. The first is attainable; the second is not.

☑ Stop thinking in terms of absolutes and consider the costs and benefits of what you're doing.

☑ Write out notes for a short lecture on why people can't be perfect. Act on your own ideas.

☑ Allow yourself to do some things less than perfectly. Ask others about the results. They may not notice there is a problem.

☑ Realize that striving for perfection is a terrible time-waster. All the time you're trying to perfect something you could be using for something better.

☑ Recognize that 80 percent of the results are usually in the first draft. Instead of trying to get the other 20 percent, spend the same time to produce another 80 percent result on a different task.

☑ Break some of the "rules" you were taught. For example, maybe it's okay to play before you do your work.

☑ Do things imperfectly; maybe even do some things imperfectly on purpose.

☑ Ann McGee-Cooper: "If you only do things you can do perfectly, you stop learning new skills, stop taking chances, and stop having fun."

PERSONAL

You are unique, and your time management system should reflect that uniqueness.

☑ Traditional time management advice is left-brain... focused on productivity and efficiency. It encourages thinking and planning in monochronic time; ignores the need for recreation and play time; and assumes that problems are solved on a logical, conscious level. Sometimes this advice is good, and sometimes it is misinformed.

☑ Recognize that there is a time to be left-brained and a time to be right-brained; a time to be efficient and a time to be creative; a time to work and a time to play; a time to be monochronic and a time to be polychronic; a time to be logical and a time to be nonlogical. One condition is not better than another, just different. Practice all of these, and learn to recognize when each is best.

☑ Left-brain thinking favors logic, detailed planning, predictability, attention to details, promptness, neatness, doing one thing at a time, and reading the instructions first before starting to assemble anything.

☑ Right-brain thinking favors variety, emotion, playfulness, surprises, planning as you go, spontaneity, creativity, intuition, playing hunches, working on several things at once, and reading the instructions only if something goes wrong.

☑ Monochronic people usually do one thing at a time, concentrate on the job at hand, adhere rigidly to plans, think in a linear progression, and can only hold one thought at a time.

☑ Polychronic people usually do many things at once, are highly distractable, change plans often and easily, think in circles all over the place, and can handle several different thoughts at a time.

☑ Convergent thinkers zero in on one solution, work step-by-step, narrow options down, are logical, like certainty, prefer facts and hard data, seek one right answer, and often appear narrow-minded to others.

☑ Divergent thinkers scan the big picture, skip around, branch out, are intuitive, look for lots of solutions, are comfortable with ambiguity, use intuition and play hunches, and often appear scatterbrained to others.

☑ To bring out your right-brain side, make fun lists, draw pictures, stick little Post-it® Notes on a sheet of paper, use different colors, use funny paper, write on a slant from corner to corner, stick small Post-it® Notes on a plastic clipboard with the most important ones on top.

☑ Use the concept of planned spontaneity. For example, set aside one afternoon for yourself; build it into your schedule. When the time arrives, do whatever you feel like doing.

☑ Give yourself permission to play. Each day should have some discipline and order and some play and foolishness.

☑ Spend at least 30 minutes every day on a high-priority personal activity that has nothing to do with work.

☑ Learn to relax and do nothing. Watch the birds in the backyard. Empty your mind.

☑ Lao Tzu: "Practice not-doing and everything will fall into place."

☑ The more we work, the more tired we get, the less creative or open-minded we are, and the less we accomplish, so we get further behind and then think we have no time for play.

☑ Worth reading: *Time Management for Unmanageable People* (Bantam, 1994) by Ann McGee-Cooper, with Duane Trammell. This book talks about time management issues from a right-brain, polychronic point of view.

PLANNING

Planning makes sure that you're ready for good results to happen.

☑ Robert Henry: "You can't no more do what you ain't prepared for than you can come back from where you ain't been."

☑ To improve your planning, ask seven questions. (1) What results do I intend to achieve? (2) What must I do to get those results? (3) What are the priorities? (4) How much time will each activity require? (5) When will I do each activity? (6) Have I allowed time for the unexpected things I can't control? (7) Who should I coordinate these activities with?

☑ Flexibility is the key to successful planning and scheduling. Allow time for the unexpected things you can't control, like interruptions, problems, or crises.

☑ Planning does not prevent daily emergencies. They will occur with or without a plan. When they do occur, emergencies do not disrupt the plan; they only disrupt the schedule.

☑ Be slow to alter your plans, even when the unexpected strikes. A thoughtful response is usually better than just reacting to events.

☑ Before you automatically agree to do anything, ask yourself if you should do it, why you should do it and when you will be able to do it, and what you will have to give up to do it.

☑ Write out a plan for every week. An excellent time to do this is on Friday afternoon before you leave for the weekend. Ask other people to do the same thing. Meet with key people to review their plans for next week and coordinate priorities and activities.

☑ Try using large wall calendars for joint planning. Use a different color for each person.

☑ Develop a systematic follow-up system. Use tickler files. Transfer to-do items to your daily planner.

☑ Learn to control your unplanned action impulses. Don't chase every unscheduled action that comes your way.

☑ Move unfinished actions to another day. Don't turn the page for tomorrow without moving unfinished items to another date. Otherwise, you'll forget all about them once you turn the page.

WEEKLY PLANNER

NAME	WEEK BEGINNING

GOALS: RESULTS TO ACHIEVE THIS WEEK

MUST DO THIS WEEK	PR	TIME NEEDED	MONDAY
			TUESDAY
			WEDNESDAY
			THURSDAY
WOULD LIKE TO DO THIS WEEK	PR	TIME NEEDED	FRIDAY
			SAT./SUN.

☑ Review your daily to-do list many times during the day. It will make it much easier for you to sort out all the things that come your way.

☑ Plan tomorrow's agenda and to-do list before you leave work today. Pull out material you will need first thing in the morning. Put items in your briefcase for early morning meetings.

☑ Give yourself more time than you think you'll need. Most of us are hopelessly optimistic about how much we can get done in a given time span.

☑ Do things the right way the first time and you won't have to find time to do them over later.

☑ Beware of Murphy's Laws: (1) Nothing is as simple as it seems; (2) Everything takes longer than you think it will; (3) If anything can go wrong, it will. Good planning minimizes the Murphy risk.

☑ Write out a daily to-do list or daily plan and consider your priorities carefully.

☑ Using an appointment book will help you to avoid overscheduling.

☑ Compare what you planned to do during the day with what you actually did during the day. You'll soon become a more realistic planner.

☑ Take care of the activities and results come out okay. You don't do a result, you do activities. Results are the end product. Focus on the right activities and the results are nearly automatic.

DAILY PRIORITY PLANNER

A1 IMPORTANT AND URGENT	B1 URGENT, NOT IMPORTANT	SCHEDULE
		6:00
		7:00
		8:00
		9:00
		10:00
		11:00
A2 IMPORTANT, NOT URGENT	**OTHER**	12:00
		1:00
		2:00
		3:00
		4:00
NOTES	**NOTES**	5:00
		6:00
		7:00
		8:00

☑ Estimating required time is also handy when delegating tasks to other people.

☑ C. Northcote Parkinson said, "Too many people find their workloads heavy because they're unable to schedule, evaluate, and coordinate their daily tasks. They keep themselves loaded with, or diverted by, that which in actuality is trivial."

☑ Use the Principle of One More: Try squeezing in just one more to-do item in your day. For example, how can you make one more call today?

☑ Set time limits and force yourself to finish jobs within those limits.

☑ Every job you have involves a series of assignments. Define the assignment clearly. Keep dated notes. Avoid unreasonable deadlines. Read every word if the assignment is written. Be flexible in planning your assignment.

PRIORITIES

GIMME AN "A"!

Pick your priorities very carefully.

☑ Think carefully about what priorities mean to you...about how you decide what is really important. Remember, you will never have enough time for everything, but you will always have time for the most important things.

☑ Trust in the truth of Pareto's Principle: "The critical elements in a set usually constitute a minority of the set."

☑ The 80-20 rule is similar to Pareto's Principle: Eighty percent of the value is in 20 percent of the items, and 20 percent of the value is in 80 percent of the items. For example, 80 percent of the sales probably comes from 20 percent of the customers.

☑ Most people start with the quick, easy, or enjoyable tasks. Instead, start with the most important tasks.

☑ Important activities are those which help you achieve your goals.

☑ Learn to distinguish between important and urgent. Any activity falls into one of four categories: (1) important and urgent, (2) important but not urgent, (3) urgent but not important, (4) neither important nor urgent. The highest payoffs and greatest opportunities are usually important but not urgent.

☑ Just because something is urgent doesn't mean it is important.

☑ Most of us have learned to respond to urgent activities but not necessarily to important activities. Don't let urgent things always take precedence over important things.

☑ Don't ignore activities which are important but not urgent. If you do, they will escalate to become urgent and important, and you'll have another crisis on your hands.

☑ Use priority codes to show both importance and urgency.

☑ Identify the importance and urgency of issues that you plan to tackle each day.

☑ Chinese proverb: Besides the noble art of getting things done, there is the noble art of leaving things undone. The wisdom of life lies in eliminating the nonessentials.

☑ Try making a "not-to-do" list as well as a "to-do" list. This will remind you not to waste time on unimportant activities.

☑ Don't always do someone else's requests at the expense of your own top-priority tasks. Learn to say no. Do it logically, firmly, and tactfully.

☑ Don't constantly switch your priorities just because people make loud demands. Be very careful about which squeaky wheels get greased.

☑ If you have any of the following common priority habits, change your ways. ✔Doing what you like to do before you do what you don't like to do. ✔Doing easy jobs before hard jobs. ✔Doing quick tasks before time-consuming tasks. ✔Responding to the demands of others before your own demands. ✔Doing urgent things before important things. ✔Waiting until the deadline approaches to get started. ✔Doing interesting jobs before uninteresting jobs. ✔Doing jobs people holler for the loudest. ✔Doing things that provide immediate closure. ✔Doing small jobs before large jobs.

☑ Personal priorities can sometimes conflict with work priorities. Be sure you know how to tell them apart.

☑ Ask yourself: "What is the most important thing I must do tomorrow?" Do your best to start with that task.

☑ Realize that despite what you say is important to you, what you do reflects your true choices and priorities.

PROCRASTINATION

Do it now! Turn your do-it-later urge into a do-it-now habit.

☑ Robert Benchley: "Anyone can do any amount of work, provided it isn't the work he is supposed to be doing at that moment."

☑ Do the most unpleasant or toughest task first.

☑ Consider the cost and benefits of delay. Hard jobs are often the easy ones you didn't do at the proper time.

☑ Tackle unpleasant jobs in small pieces and short time segments. Break the task into a set of minijobs.

☑ Promise yourself a reward for completing the task. If you earn the reward, be sure to take it. If you don't earn the reward, don't take it.

☑ Try thinking of the task in a larger context. Think about how you will benefit by doing the task. It may make it more palatable.

☑ Delegate the task to someone else who may enjoy doing it. Just because you don't enjoy a particular task doesn't mean that other people won't like it either. Others often enjoy what we don't like to do.

☑ Break complex tasks down into smaller steps. Focus on one step at a time.

☑ Do a small, leading task that will get you moving in the right direction.

☑ Give yourself a pep talk. Feeling sorry for yourself is not justification for putting things off.

☑ Disinterest often results when you are familiar with something. Learn more about the task. Information is often the key to movement.

☑ Don't be a perfectionist. You are paid to get results, not to be perfect. Learn when it is good enough to get the desired results.

☑ Keep a list of all the things you tend to worry about. Go back over the list from time to time and see how many of your worries came true.

☑ When you're procrastinating, simply admit it. Stop rationalizing and making excuses. You're only fooling yourself.

☑ Don't wait for the right mood. Start in spite of your mood. Thomas Edison said that creativity is 99 percent perspiration and only 1 percent inspiration.

☑ Commit yourself to action. Set deadlines. Promise results to others. Fear of losing face is a powerful motivator.

☑ Indecision is often a form of procrastination. Don't invest more time and energy in a decision than it is worth.

☑ The very thought of having more to get done than you appear to have time to do can paralyze your will. Stop thinking about it and do something.

☑ Start with what you have.

☑ Start your thinking at the finished result, and then work backward to break jobs down into subunits.

☑ After you have divided large tasks into smaller ones, add milestones so you will be aware of progress.

☑ Make radical changes to your routines.

☑ There's a big difference between dreaming and doing. Stop dreaming and start doing.

PROJECTS

Planning a project involves thinking about the future in a systematic manner.

☑ Even the small, ordinary, everyday kind of projects should be carefully planned, such as a seminar teaching people how to use a new telephone system or cleaning out your garage. If the job in mind has several steps, it's probably a project. Even simple things that you do all by yourself will get done faster and go smoother if you take a little time to plan out all the steps.

☑ When you're planning a project, ask questions about potential problems: What are the critical points? What is most likely to go wrong? How and when will I know? What will I do about it?

☑ Identify all the activities that must be done to complete the project. Estimate the time needed for each activity. Decide when each activity must be started and completed

PROJECT PLANNER

NAME	DATE CREATED	DUE DATE

PROJECT TEAM MEMBERS

PROJECT OBJECTIVES— INTENDED RESULTS

BACKGROUND INFORMATION — MIND MAP — DIAGRAMS — NOTES

to keep things on schedule. Decide who will be responsible for each activity and what special resources they may need.

☑ Schedule activities on major projects before they become urgent. Place notes in your tickler file reminding you to act on each of the key activities in a timely fashion.

☑ When considering the timing of activities, think about a starting time that will give you enough slack to allow for problems along the way and avoid last-minute rush jobs.

☑ Don't ignore the deadlines you set for yourself. Treat your own deadlines with as much respect as you would treat deadlines from your boss.

☑ Learn to use simple Gantt charts to display the time dimensions of a project. (1) List activities in sequence down the left side of the chart. (2) List time intervals across the top or bottom of the chart. (3) Draw a line across the chart for each activity. The line starts at the beginning time for the activity and ends at the time that activity should be completed.

☑ A simple Gantt activity-time chart will show the total time required for the project, the sequence of each activity, and which activities can be done at the same time. This is an excellent way to show others what you plan to do and how the parts are related to each other. It also helps you keep things under control.

PROJECT PLANNER—KEY ACTIVITIES

PROJECT NAME		DATE CREATED		DUE DATE	

PROJECT OBJECTIVES— INTENDED RESULTS

KEY PROJECT ACTIVITIES	TIME NEEDED	START DATE	DUE DATE	PERSON RESPONSIBLE	RESOURCES NEEDED

QUESTIONS

**Asking the right questions
can be one of the best
time management techniques.**

☑ Don't assume anything. Ask questions to find out for sure.

☑ Use questions to keep meetings on track.

☑ Avoid closed-end questions and negative questions.

☑ Ask questions that require more than single-word answers. Can you give me more detail? Can you give me an example? What does that mean to me? How did you come to that conclusion?

☑ Bible, Matthew 7:7: Ask and it will be given to you; seek and you will find; knock and the door will be opened to you.

☑ Edward Dayton suggests asking thought-provoking questions. Ask why and you may eliminate it. Ask where and you may find a better place for it. Ask when and you may find a better schedule. Ask who and you are likely to find the most appropriate person to do it. Ask what and you may find you are working on the wrong problem. Ask how and you may find a better solution.

QUIET TIME

**Everyone needs some quiet time
to get important work done.**

☑ Create some quiet time for yourself during the day. Make yourself unavailable for an hour or so in the morning and maybe again in the afternoon. Close your door, or go hide somewhere.

☑ Use lights, signs, flags, or something to indicate your availability to people. Most will respect your wishes.

☑ Close your door for some quiet time, but don't abuse it. Although you are entitled to uninterrupted time, you must also be available to others who need you. Try scheduling regular times to see key people.

☑ Establish quiet hours during which you accept only emergency calls.

☑ To increase your productivity, try for an hour of uninterrupted work first thing in the morning.

☑ Don't isolate yourself too much; there's no substitute for personal interaction.

☑ Yes, you can find quiet time, if you really try.

☑ Establish a company quiet time policy, where everyone gets an uninterrupted hour at the same time. It can work miracles for your company.

☑ Call Barbara Fulton, VP of Administration at Michigan Millers Mutual Insurance Company at 517-482-6211. They've used company quiet time for over 35 years. Ask her how well quiet time has worked for them and how they administer it.

☑ Remember that quiet time is designed to hold off internal interruptions, not customers. When customers call, be sure to take care of them.

QUOTES

Time is a paradox: You never seem to have enough time, yet you have all the time there is.

- ☑ Peter Drucker: "Time is basic; unless it is managed, nothing else can be managed."

- ☑ Ben Franklin: "Time is money."

- ☑ Anonymous: "Press on. Nothing in the world can take the place of persistence. Talent will not; nothing is more common than unsuccessful men with talent. Genius will not; unrewarded genius is almost a proverb. Education will not; the world is full of educated derelicts. Persistence and determination alone are omnipotent."

- ☑ Howard Hunt: "There are two rules for achieving anything. Rule No. 1: Get started. Rule No. 2: Keep going."

- ☑ Sidney Harris: "Winners focus, losers spray."

☑ Voltaire: "Time is man's most precious asset. All men neglect it; all regret the loss of it; nothing can be done without it."

☑ James McCay: "Nothing ever happens in your life unless you create the space for it to happen in."

☑ Proverb: "The more you do of what you're doing, the more you'll get of what you're getting."

☑ Robert Schuller: "There's a price for every prize. Everyone wants the prize, but no one wants to pay the price."

☑ Alan Cimberg: "If it is to be, it is up to me."

☑ Kenneth McFarlane: "Spectacular performance is usually preceded by unspectacular preparation."

☑ Chinese proverb: "Besides the noble art of getting things done, there is the noble art of leaving things undone. The wisdom of life lies in eliminating the nonessentials."

☑ Peter Drucker: "Most people are more concerned with doing things right than with doing the right things. The secret is to focus on doing the right things right."

☑ Earl Nightingale: "Habits are the key to top performance. Winners form the habit of doing the things that losers don't like to do."

☑ Merrill Douglass: "Time management is a way of working and living, realizing that we're each responsible for our own results."

☑ Fortune cookie: "When nothing is pressing, putter around with this or that."

☑ Proverb: "The time you enjoy wasting may not be a waste of time."

☑ Arthur Schopenhauer: "Ordinary people think merely how they will *spend* time; a man of intellect tries to *use* it."

☑ Oliver Wendell Holmes, Jr.: "A mind stretched to a new idea never goes back to its original dimensions."

READING

Be selective about what you read, and build good reading skills.

☑ Get off junk circulation lists. Cancel unnecessary subscriptions.

☑ Share the reading with others, especially if you all have to read the same material. Each of you could do part of the reading and share the highlights of what you read with each other.

☑ Use summaries, which are faster to read. You can develop your own summaries, and you can buy prepared summaries. Ask others to include summaries of their reports at the front.

☑ For excellent summaries of current business books, contact Soundview Executive Book Summaries, 5 Main Street, Bristol, VT 05443; 800-521-1227.

☑ Record some material on tape instead of putting everything on paper. You can listen at times when you can't read. For instance, the average American worker spends about two hours daily commuting to and from work.

☑ To buy or rent books on tape, contact Books On Tape, Inc., P.O. Box 7900, Newport Beach, CA 92685; 800-626-3333.

☑ Use tape recorders that allow you to listen to a tape at twice the recorded speed. You will get the message in half the time. Go by a Radio Shack store and ask to see Model 14-1052, which allows up to a 200 percent speed increase and has a separate adjustment for pitch to get rid of the chipmunk effect.

☑ The general rule for periodicals is to never keep an issue for more than two cycles. You should throw out the previous issue when the issue after next arrives. That means that newspapers wouldn't be kept for more than two days; weekly magazines for more than two weeks; monthly magazines for more than two months.

☑ Set up a reading file. Rip out articles you're interested in and put them in the file. Take the file with you on trips.

☑ To speed up magazine reading: look at contents, circle items of interest, rip out the articles, throw the rest of the magazine out.

☑ Instead of circulating the whole magazine, circulate a copy of the table of contents. Send copies of any articles people want to see.

☑ To speed up newspaper reading: flip page by page, glance at the headlines, read the first line or two of articles, circle or highlight the article if it looks important, read the most important articles now, tear out other articles for reading later.

☑ Read at home, read while you travel, read while you wait, read at lunchtime or breaks. Always carry reading material with you.

☑ Scan the table of contents in magazines to see if there is anything you're really interested in. If not, throw the magazine out.

☑ Read the book jacket and the table of contents before deciding to read the book. Check the beginning and end of chapters; look for summary chapters first. Read the preface and introduction before starting the rest of the book.

☑ If you rip out a page to send to someone else, send it or fax it immediately. If you fax the page, then throw the original away as soon as you've faxed it.

☑ Make notes in the margins while you're reading. Don't hesitate to mark pages freely.

☑ Do your most important reading when your mind is alert.

☑ You can read early editions of newspapers the night before.

☑ Read before going to sleep every night. Get a special pair of glasses for reading in bed. When you're reclining in bed, your book is farther from your eyes than when you're sitting up.

☑ Read with a purpose, not aimlessly.

☑ Pause and summarize. Ask yourself what you have just been reading. Put it into your own words.

☑ Skip unimportant parts.

☑ Look up unfamiliar words. When you encounter a word you don't know, your mind stops for the next several sentences.

☑ Bunch reading material. For instance, try to go through six magazines in twenty minutes, rather than just one. This is an application of Parkinson's Law: Work expands to fill the time available.

☑ Learn to read faster. The average adult only reads about 200 words per minute. With a little effort, you can triple or even quadruple your reading speed.

SAYING NO

No!
Non!
Nein!
¡No!

**Practice saying no
until you get good at it.**

☑ Be assertive, and say no when you should.

☑ Look for ways to say no objectively. People accept an objective response better than a subjective response.

☑ Learn to say no positively, tactfully, and firmly.

☑ Let your secretary, your boss, or someone else say no for you. Others will accept it better and won't argue with you about it.

☑ Refer to your schedule before you consider your response. Say no if it won't fit.

☑ Tell people why you must say no to their request.

☑ Provide them with options, if possible. However, don't shove your problems off on someone else.

☑ If it is your boss, ask what you should set aside in order to take on the new task.

Don't say maybe, say no. Be gracious, but be firm.

 Don't feel obligated or guilty. It is okay to say no to some requests. Resist attempts to manipulate or intimidate you.

SCHEDULING

Things that are scheduled are more likely to happen.

☑ Schedule the most important activities for each day. Things that are scheduled are much more likely to happen.

☑ Keep a record of what you scheduled and what you actually did at those times. Comparing the two will help you discover ways to schedule more realistically.

☑ Learn to control your unscheduled action impulses. Don't chase after unimportant actions just because they pop up during the day.

☑ Use large time blocks for important work. Schedule quiet time so you can work without interruption.

☑ Meet with your secretary or assistant for a few minutes every morning to review objectives, priorities, and planned actions for the day. A brief afternoon meeting may also help keep things in focus and make necessary adjustments in your schedule.

☑ Ask your secretary or assistant to help you plan and schedule your time. You might even want to turn some of the scheduling over to your secretary.

☑ Prepare tomorrow's schedule before you leave work today. You'll sleep better, and you won't risk starting your day by reacting before you consider what is really important.

☑ Identify your prime time, the time of day when you are at your best, when you do your best work. Try to set this time aside for important projects, making important decisions, or doing creative work.

☑ When making out your schedule, be sure to allow enough time for each activity. Most people are overly optimistic. They don't allow enough time and they often start late. As a result, their jobs are more frantic and pressured than need be.

☑ Group related items and actions whenever possible.

☑ Remember Parkinson's Law: Work expands to fill the time available. If you allow more time than you actually need, you'll use everything you've allowed anyway.

☑ The opposite of allowing too much time is not allowing enough. That's Murphy's Second Law: Everything takes longer than you think it will.

☑ Your challenge is to schedule enough time for your activities but not too much. Set time limits for everything you do. Try to finish within the time allowed.

☑ Whenever possible, set appointments to see people. Call ahead and confirm that they will be there.

☑ Schedule appointments with yourself to happen as quickly as an appointment for someone else. Actually write yourself in on the calendar.

☑ Do important work as early in the day as possible. Take care of routine and firefighting tasks the rest of the day.

☑ Don't schedule appointments for early in the morning. Keep this time for working without interruption on your most important tasks. If someone asks for an early hour, tell her or him you have a conflict and suggest another time.

☑ When you're planning back-to-back appointments, don't forget to consider how long it may take you to get from one place to another. If you're driving, for instance, the time of day could be critical.

☑ It's always a good idea to allow yourself a safety valve. Assume that meetings will take at least 50 percent longer than you expect.

☑ Always allow yourself a 15-minute cushion between meetings or appointments.

☑ Schedule specific times for little jobs, after you've completed more important work.

☑ People often forget about Monday morning meetings. Call Friday to remind them.

☑ If you're running late for meetings or appointments, call to say so.

☑ When making appointments for early morning, Monday morning, or out of town, get the person's home number.

☑ Arrive at appointments 5 to 10 minutes early.

☑ If you must do activities involving other people, try to schedule them early in the day.

☑ Use color to highlight activities in your schedule, notebook, etc. For instance, regular appointments with key staff could be highlighted in red.

☑ Tackle big jobs first thing in the morning. Don't waste that time on newspapers, coffee, conversations, or other trivial matters.

☑ Don't become a slave to the clock, squelching individual uniqueness and creativity in favor of speed or schedules.

☑ Schedule play and time off as seriously as you schedule work. Too much work and too little play is not good for anyone.

SECRETARIES

"We're a team, Ms. Phyltz"

Consider your secretary as an important member of your team.

☑ Take time to discuss team effectiveness, how both of you can use time better.

☑ Treat your secretary with dignity and respect. Provide support and backup.

☑ Discuss goals, priorities, and plans with your secretary daily. Do it first thing every morning.

☑ Don't interrupt your secretary so much during the day. Bunch things together. Go easy on the intercom buzzer, too.

☑ Coordinate activities with your secretary so both of you can get as much done as possible.

☑ Provide as much lead time as you can. Avoid last-minute rush jobs.

☑ Discuss problems and ideas with your secretary. Ask your secretary for ideas and suggestions.

- ☑ Provide your secretary with the best office equipment available.

- ☑ Allow your secretary to organize you and your office procedures.

- ☑ Tell your secretary where you are going, how you can be reached, and when you will return.

- ☑ Keep your secretary fully informed about what is happening. Ask what he or she would like to know about your business, projects, goals, and priorities.

- ☑ Expect the best. Provide for your secretary's professional development. Include your secretary in training and development programs.

- ☑ Encourage other people to deal directly with your secretary on routine matters.

- ☑ Don't expect a shared secretary to resolve the problems of working for multiple bosses. That's your responsibility.

- ☑ Ask your secretary how you could manage your time better and what he or she could do that you are now doing.

- ☑ Discuss the major timewasters that bother you and your secretary, and what you could do to resolve them.

- ☑ Take time to provide clear instructions and complete information the first time.

- ☑ Use good feedback techniques.

- ☑ Allow for individual initiative. Don't expect your secretary to do things the way you do them. And don't compare your current secretary to your previous secretary.

☑ Tell your secretary what you expect, but be sure that what you expect is reasonable.

☑ Build on your secretary's strengths and overlook the weaknesses.

☑ Handle any reprimands in private, and never criticize your secretary to other people.

☑ Protect your secretary's time. Help your secretary find quiet time regularly. You can run interference or block drop-ins on some occasions.

☑ Develop a sense of humor. Seeing the humor in things helps build smooth working relationships.

SIMPLIFYING

**Things complicate life.
The more you have, the more
they have you. Less is more.
Slower is better. Simple is great.**

☑ Lao-tzu: "He who knows enough is enough will always have enough."

☑ Clean everything out of your house or apartment. Keep only the essentials. Get used to the "bare" look.

☑ Stop accumulating things just because everyone else is doing it. Do you really need it? How will it make your life better?

☑ The more things you have, the less value you have for any one of them. You wind up having so many things you have no value for any of them.

☑ Spend less time accumulating money and things; spend more time building relationships with people.

☑ Make a list of the things you would try to save if the house caught on fire. Pare it down to the few items which have real lasting value for you.

☑ Do some things the old-fashioned slow way.

☑ Give things away to people who need them or who can truly use them.

☑ Learn to be satisfied with what you have.

☑ Move into a smaller house. You'll have less to clean and maintain. Move to an apartment or condo and you may gain even more.

☑ Don't buy clothes that need to be dry-cleaned or ironed.

☑ Buy in bulk: groceries, toiletries, underwear, socks, etc. You spend less time shopping and washing.

☑ Visit a monastery or convent. Think about how life there is simpler and easier than yours is. Imagine how you could get closer to their way of life.

☑ Create a simpler wardrobe. Concentrate on a few colors and styles that look really good on you.

☑ Make a list of the things and people who add the most pleasure to your life. Do the things you enjoy with the people you enjoy. Most of them also cost very little.

☑ Turn off the TV. Spend time reading, playing games, conversing, and just relaxing with no agenda. If the TV or the VCR breaks, don't fix it.

☑ Cancel magazine and newspaper subscriptions. Drop call waiting. Open the mail only once a week. Get rid of your car phone.

☑ Make gifts instead of buying them. Be creative. Only give gifts that can be read or eaten.

☑ Get out of debt. Live on half your income. Don't buy something you can get along without. Keep only one credit card, and use it for emergencies only. Never shop on impulse.

☑ Consolidate your investments. Have only one checking account.

☑ Move closer to work, or consider working where you live.

☑ Eat less and eat lean.

☑ Sell your exercise equipment, cancel your health club memberships, and fire your personal trainer. Go for long walks regularly.

☑ Leave earlier; drive slower; don't change lanes so often.

☑ On the weekends, only do things you enjoy.

☑ Learn to trust your intuition. Get out of relationships that aren't good for you.

☑ Stop trying to change other people. Be yourself and let others be themselves. Concentrate on the positives.

☑ Learn to enjoy solitude. Go on a retreat at least once every year.

☑ Say no to things you don't need, to activities you don't want to do, to anything that tends to complicate your life.

☑ Keep a journal. Review your life regularly and think about ways to simplify it.

☑ Change your expectations.

☑ Try "speed cleaning" your house instead of "deep cleaning" it.

☑ Leave the office for lunch every day, even if all you do is walk around the block.

☑ There is no point in looking for ways to save more time just to do more things faster. Think about doing fewer things that add more satisfaction.

☑ Learn to be more self-sufficient. Do things yourself instead of hiring someone to do them.

☑ Make a list of the things that really matter and spend more time on those things. Drop everything else.

☑ Celebrate the ordinary; it may be more important than what we call significant stuff.

SLEEP

When you're rested,
you think better and work better.

☑ Get up when you wake up.

☑ If you arise fresh, without the need for an alarm clock, you have had sufficient rest. If you have to force yourself to get up, you probably need more sleep.

☑ Don't eat a big, heavy meal too close to bedtime.

☑ Soak in a warm bath—100 degrees—before bedtime.

☑ Carefully stretch and relax every muscle in the body.

☑ Eliminate noise in your bedroom. A fan in the room helps.

☑ Don't argue with your spouse just before bedtime.

☑ Avoid stimulants for at least six hours before bedtime.

☑ Set regular times for going to bed and getting up.

☑ Leave at least an hour or two to unwind before going to bed. You can't work right up to bedtime and expect to fall asleep quickly.

☑ Watching television in bed makes it more difficult to have a good night's sleep. Instead of watching TV, try reading or listening to relaxing music just before bedtime.

☑ Regular daily exercise helps you sleep better.

☑ If you can't sleep, get up, go somewhere else, turn on a light, read something boring. Go back to bed when you feel sleepy.

☑ Avoid sleeping pills. It's better to rearrange your lifestyle and change your habits.

☑ If you feel tired, you are not necessarily lacking sleep. Being tired is just as often a symptom of stress, depression, or poor nutrition, none of which will be solved by sleeping more.

☑ If you can't get enough sleep at night, try taking naps during the day. Lunch or breaks are good times for this. You can learn to put your head on your desk and sleep for 15 to 20 minutes, then wake up, with or without an alarm clock. With today's hectic pace, many people are rediscovering the value of naps.

SOCIALIZING

**Socializing is like aspirin:
A little helps a lot, but too much
can be deadly.**

☑ Socializing helps build positive relationships. However, too much socializing is a huge timewaster and prevents achievement.

☑ Don't rationalize that all conversations are somehow worthwhile. Just because you're talking doesn't mean you're building relationships.

☑ Unnecessary socializing may stem from habit, ego, curiosity, desire to be liked, or even from procrastination. Learn to recognize your actions for what they are.

☑ Look for ways to reduce socializing without becoming antisocial.

☑ Make time available to talk with people, but don't waste time chatting when you should be working.

☑ Don't wander around and chit-chat with people too much. Add a little more structure and purpose to your interactions.

☑ When you talk business with others, don't waste time with unnecessary small talk. Learn to get to your point quickly. People don't need to know everything you know.

STAFF

Treat other people the way you would like to be treated; the results are terrific.

- ☑ Managers exist to facilitate performance. Subordinates are not here to serve superiors; superiors are here to serve subordinates.

- ☑ W.C. Fields said, "You can't push a piece of cooked spaghetti very far, but you can pull it forever."

- ☑ Set a good example for others to follow.

- ☑ Meet with your secretary, administrative assistant, or other key people to review your plans and priorities. People can't help you unless they know what you're trying to do.

- ☑ Delegate as much as you can to your staff. This will free you up to handle things only you can do.

- ☑ Consider having people tape record their reports to you. This allows you the freedom of listening instead of reading. For instance, you could listen to their reports while driving to and from work. Many people actually prefer this kind of reporting.

☑ Learn to adjust to different personalities and work styles; everyone is different, and that's okay.

☑ Realize that you need to focus on both productive results and positive relationships. If you emphasize either one at the expense of the other, you will develop problems.

☑ Show people you respect them and their time: Don't waste their time, don't constantly interrupt them, and don't make them wait on you.

☑ Set a good example for your staff by being a good time manager yourself. Don't expect them to manage their time well if you're not managing your time well.

☑ Take time to properly train and develop staff people; it's a key part of your job.

☑ Keep everyone informed about what is happening—changes in objectives, plans, priorities, thinking.

☑ Examine work flow in your area and look for ways to simplify the work for everyone. Involve your staff in brainstorming to generate ideas.

☑ At least once a month, ask staff people how you waste their time or hinder their progress. Change your ways.

☑ Develop a continuing dialogue about how to use time well and minimize common timewasters.

☑ Do a group time analysis and share the results with everyone. Ask for ideas on how to improve conditions.

☑ Spend time building people up rather than putting them down.

☑ Take the time to give people clear instructions and complete information the first time. It will save an enormous amount of time and prevent many mistakes.

☑ Develop the on-time habit: Be on time for meetings and appointments, deliver work to people on time, meet promised deadlines. Encourage everyone on your staff to do the same.

☑ Practice the Golden Rule: Treat other people the way you would like to be treated. The results are terrific.

☑ On Friday afternoon, ask everyone on your staff to prepare a weekly plan. Then, before leaving for the weekend, get together to share each other's plans and coordinate activities. You'll all be ready for a productive start on Monday morning.

☑ Discuss how people who work closely together waste each other's time. Look for ways to work together better.

☑ Make a discussion of time use part of the regular performance review and set improvement objectives.

☑ Use the last few minutes of each staff meeting to discuss how to use group time better.

STRESS

There are two rules for stress-free living:
(1) Don't sweat the small stuff.
(2) Realize that it's all small stuff.

☑ In a recent study, about half of all companies reported they were understaffed. As a result, two-thirds of them reported increased stress and 40 percent reported difficulty meeting schedules and deadlines.

☑ Stress is any action or situation that places special physical or psychological demands on you. Too little stress—and too much stress—is bad for performance.

☑ If you're wound up tight by day's end, try a massage, a warm soak in the tub, or the whirlpool.

☑ Get plenty of rest. Your body needs time to restore itself.

☑ Watch your diet. Eat healthy foods. Minimize sugar, salt, fat, cholesterol, caffeine, and alcohol.

☑ Exercise regularly. You need at least 20 minutes of rigorous exercise every other day. Walking is an excellent way to exercise.

☑ Learn to relax. Think relaxed. Work relaxed. Live relaxed. To be sure you really are relaxed, you can use a GSR device that measures sweat-gland activity.

☑ Two major job stress factors are having a bad boss and not being able to control the work pace. A bad boss is the worst of the two. Try to avoid both conditions.

☑ Find a job that is interesting, challenging, or enjoyable, or one you really care about.

☑ Nurture relationships. Get to know people well. Talk with them. Laugh with them. Share their concerns. Talk things over with others instead of bottling them up inside.

☑ Change your job to reduce the stress level. Improved procedures, greater authority, and more involvement can make a big difference.

☑ Take short naps during the day. A nap may do you more good than a coffee break.

☑ Take breaks. When you feel yourself tensing up, leave the situation. Or take a few minutes off and play humorous tapes that make you laugh.

☑ Listen to good music. Choose music with no lyrics, music that's familiar, music with no emotional baggage, and music with harmonic chord structures. Sixty-cycle music is especially good because it automatically produces an alpha wave in your brain that helps you relax better.

☑ Learn healthy ways to dissipate your anger. When you feel like hitting someone, beat up on a punching bag. The Hitman Home Boxercise Unit is a great punching bag that fits nicely into your home or office. Contact NDL Products, Inc., 4031 NE 12th Terrace, Oakland Park, FL 33334; 800-979-4343.

☑ Develop hobbies that interest you.

☑ Take regular vacations.

☑ Take up gardening.

☑ Fine-tune your living environment. Choose soothing colors for the walls, use incandescent lighting or full-spectrum fluorescent lighting, install dimmer switches so you can adjust light levels, use sound absorbing materials, arrange furniture around relaxing focal points, add plants, keep the temperature comfortable.

☑ Read a good book on stress management. Attend a stress management seminar.

☑ Develop productive ways to release tension.

☑ Laugh more. Laughter is good for you. Listen to humorous tapes.

☑ Slow down. Don't be in such a big hurry. Try to control the pace of your work, if you can. React slower. Eat slower, talk slower, walk slower.

☑ Change your attitude. Positive thinkers handle stress much better.

☑ Take time to relax and recharge your body and mind.

☑ Learn to look at things from a long-term perspective. What difference will it make five years from now?

☑ Try using NoiseBuster headphones. Instead of drowning out background noise, they neutralize the noise by creating antinoise, a mirror image of the background noise. For NoiseBuster Personal Active Noise Reduction Headphones, contact Noise Cancellation Technologies, Inc., 1025 W. Nursery Road, Linthicum, MD 21090; 800-278-3526.

☑ Recite the Serenity Prayer often: "God, grant me the serenity to accept the things I cannot change, courage to change the things I can, and wisdom to know the difference."

TEAMWORK

Think of others first; look for ways to save time and effort for the people you work with.

☑ No one accomplishes much on their own. It's up to you to develop a strong support team around you.

☑ Show people you respect them and their time.

☑ Develop the on-time habit. Show up for meetings and appointments on time; deliver work on time. Make sure that others never have to wait on you. Encourage others to do the same.

☑ Discuss objectives, priorities, and plans with your superiors, peers, and support staff. Do it often.

☑ Set aside regularly scheduled times for talking with key people. Don't just drop in spontaneously.

☑ Make an agenda before calling or meeting with anyone.

☑ Don't be in too big a hurry when instructing others. Take time to do it right. Be sure you provide complete information and clear instructions. Check to be sure they really understand everything.

☑ Take time to be a good listener. It saves lots of time and prevents many problems.

☑ Be patient. Take time to communicate effectively. It pays big dividends.

☑ Start earlier. Ask for things early. Allow more lead time. Give people plenty of advance notice. Avoid last-minute rush jobs.

☑ Make sure your expectations are reasonable.

☑ Recognize and reward good performance. Be sure to express appreciation regularly.

☑ Establish a quiet-time policy for your company or office. Help everyone concentrate on important work without constant interruptions.

☑ Ask others how you waste their time, and change anything you can.

☑ Ask everyone for ideas on how to improve everything. The more ideas you get, the more you can improve.

☑ Obey your good impulses. Be helpful to others, say something pleasant, ask questions about their interests, and show appreciation.

☑ No matter how good you are, you can't do everything. It is up to you to develop a strong support team to help everyone achieve more. None of us can do as much as all of us.

☑ Don't wait for someone else to take the first step; you move first. Assume that everything depends on you: "If it is to be, it is up to me."

☑ Involve the entire team in the planning process.

☑ Ask all team members to prepare weekly plans for their own work. Meet weekly to coordinate priorities and team activities with each other.

☑ Identify and discuss the biggest timewasters for the team. Look for ways to minimize these problems.

☑ Think about how to best use team time. Ask questions: What are we trying to achieve? What's important and what isn't? What are the priorities? What can we eliminate? How well must various functions be done? What can we simplify and streamline? What can be modified or combined? Get the entire team involved in discussing possible improvements.

☑ Have team members keep time logs of what they actually do. Combine these to see the total team time allocations. Go over results with team members and discuss how everyone could use time better.

☑ Worth reading: *Time Management for Teams* by Merrill and Donna Douglass (Amacom).

TELEPHONES

**Instead of being irritated
when the phone rings, tell yourself,
"That's my job calling!"**

☑ If you think of the telephone as your job calling, you will be less frustrated.

☑ Analyze your phone calls to determine who should answer your telephone. The higher the organizational level, the greater the risk that answering your own phone is a timewaster.

☑ Have someone screen incoming calls and offer to help callers on all routine matters.

☑ Develop a plan for screening, delegating, and consolidating calls.

☑ Train people to answer your telephone effectively. Consider what to say, how to say it, which questions to ask, how to refer callers, and how to take complete messages.

☑ Have your secretary look up answers for your return calls.

☑ Get through the small talk as quickly as possible. Get right to the point and stay there.

☑ Bring calls to a prompt close. Be firm, but don't be rude.

☑ Tell people who call you when you prefer to receive calls or when you are most likely to be in.

☑ Record and analyze your telephone calls periodically. Find out what is really happening on your telephone.

☑ Use voice mail systems or call-forwarding or answering machines when you are gone.

☑ Use a timer on your telephone; it will help you keep conversations short.

☑ Consider alternatives to phone calls, such as fax, memos, or electronic mail.

☑ Smile when you are talking on the telephone. You will convey a more positive image and get better results in less time.

☑ Stand up when you answer your telephone and you will spend less time on your calls.

☑ Plan your calls. Have information at hand. Make an agenda. Organize yourself before you call. Be prepared to talk. Unplanned calls take 57 percent more time.

☑ Group outgoing calls for greater efficiency.

☑ Tell long-winded callers that you have another call, appointment, or emergency. As a last resort, to get rid of long-winded callers, hang up...while *you* are talking.

TELEPHONE LOG OF INCOMING CALLS

DATE	TIME	DUR-ATION	PERSON CALLING	PURPOSE OF CALL— TOPICS DISCUSSED	FOLLOW-U
TOTAL CALLS				TOTAL PEOPLE	

☑ A good message includes name, number, reason for call, what you need from the person, company, time, when to call you back, when you'll call again, who the person can talk to if you're not in.

☑ To end calls quickly, try saying to the caller: "I was just walking out the door." "There's someone in my office now." "I've got a call holding on another line." or "I'm in the middle of a meeting."

☑ Schedule conference calls.

☑ Record your telephone conversations. Listen to yourself and look for ways to improve.

☑ Realize that an increasing number of people don't return calls to anyone. Go ahead and leave a message, but don't expect a return call. Call again.

☑ You don't have to answer every call. It's okay to let your voice mail system pick up calls. Use the screening feature to see who is calling. Pick up if you like.

☑ If you're on the phone constantly, try using a lightweight telephone headset. Advantages: hands free, no neck pain, easy to take notes, easy to move around, no echo for the caller. Contact Plantronics, 345 Encinal Street, Santa Cruz, CA 95060; 800-426-5858.

☑ If you're pestered with an unsolicited call, press the hold button and go about your work. See how long it takes the caller to realize you're not there.

☑ Put the caller on hold to give yourself time to think, regroup, or develop a strategy.

☑ Don't pick up someone else's phone just to be a nice guy.

☑ About half of all business calls convey one-way information. Use fax instead.

☑ If you're requesting action, make those calls early in the day, or late at night on their voice mail.

☑ Use the speaker phone when you're on hold so you can do other things while waiting. But pick up the receiver as soon as the other person comes on the line.

TELEPHONE TAG

Hi, there! It's your turn to call me!

Telephone tag can't be eliminated, but it can be minimized.

☑ Ask people you call frequently when they prefer to receive calls or when they are most likely to be in. Call at those times whenever possible.

☑ If the person you are calling is not available, ask if someone else can help you.

☑ Rather than leaving a message, you may want to call again. An increasing number of people simply don't return any phone calls.

☑ If you must leave a message, make sure it is very complete. The better the message, the better your chances of getting a callback and the response you want.

☑ To get through more often, call in the early morning, call after hours, call during lunch, ask the secretary for a direct number, and ask about preferred call times.

☑ Consider alternative times and ways to reach people. First-class mail is becoming popular again.

☑ Use call forwarding so people can get to you when you're not in your office. Beepers may also help.

☑ If possible, when you leave a message, tell the party why it's to his or her advantage to call you back.

TICKLER FILES

A good tickler file is like having an extra memory in a drawer.

☑ Use a tickler file to store material until you need it, with full confidence that you will see it again at the proper time. You can use manual tickler files, computerized tickler files, or both. These are also called bring-forward files, follow-up files, or reminder files.

☑ To create a manual tickler file, you will need 43 folders. Label one folder for each day of the month, and label one folder for each month of the year.

☑ Computerized tickler files are built into contact manager software programs, such as ACT! (Symantec Corporation, 10201 Torre Avenue, Cupertino, CA 95014; 800-441-7234).

☑ File items on the date you next want to see them.

☑ Check the current folder every day.

☑ At the end of the month, sort the items for next month into the proper day (1 to 31) file.

☑ For critical items, you may want to create an alphabetical cross-index file so you can find them at random times.

☑ Before you prepare a weekly plan, check your tickler file for the next seven days, but leave the items in the file to reinforce your habit of checking the current day-file every day.

☑ Before leaving for a trip, check to see what will come up in the tickler file while you're gone. You can either do it before you leave, take it with you, or move it to a different date.

☑ Use tickler files to help you track and remember anything: birthdays, when to change batteries in the clock, anniversaries, due dates for assignments, vacations, aging things you're not sure about (until you decide what to do with them!), etc. You are limited only by your own imagination.

TRAVEL

Plan your trip time as carefully as you plan your time in the office.

☑ Set specific goals for the trip. What results are you after? What do you want to make happen? Be realistic, too. Don't try to do too much in too short a time.

☑ Ask yourself if the trip is really necessary. What do you hope to achieve? Would a phone call or a videoconference work as well? Do you need face-to-face communication? Is there another way to get the same result?

☑ Plan your trip time as carefully as you plan your time in the office. Set priorities. Estimate how much time you will need for each activity. Allow flexibility into your schedule for unexpected problems.

☑ Pace yourself. Prepare for time zone changes. Build recovery time into your schedule. Allow for jet lag.

☑ Clarify and coordinate with people on the other end. Tell them what you expect to achieve and ask about their expectations. Help them plan and organize for your visit.

☑ Plan for off-time as well as on-time. You can't hit it hard all the time. Take pleasure books, tapes, or magazines. Travel can be both physically and psychologically exhausting. You need time to unwind, to relax, to refresh yourself.

☑ Be sensible. Don't overdo it just because you are out of town. Watch your diet. Don't eat drastically different than you usually do. If anything, you should eat less, eat blander foods, drink less, and go to bed earlier.

☑ Travel light. Plan one-color trips. Select clothes that can do double duty. Miniaturize everything you can.

☑ Check weather conditions and pack accordingly.

☑ Use carry-on cases so you won't have to check any luggage.

☑ Develop checklists, both for work materials and for personal items. You'll be less likely to forget something.

☑ Allow plenty of time between meetings for travel.

☑ Organize your briefcase like a traveling office. Be sure you have everything you will need to work on the move.

☑ Plan how to make travel time productive. Think about what you can do in airports, airplanes, hotel rooms. Turn travel time into learning time by listening to cassette tapes.

☑ Consider a laptop computer, portable fax machine, and cellular telephone to make travel time more productive.

☑ Try to finish all paperwork generated by the trip before the trip ends. You won't have to find time for it when you get back to the office.

☑ If you're traveling out of the office, try to group your appointments to minimize the time you spend driving or walking from place to place.

☑ Allow plenty of extra time if you have to travel through areas where traffic is heavy or where construction slows things down.

☑ Leave a detailed itinerary behind so people will know how to find you.

☑ Confirm appointments before you leave.

☑ Before you take a trip, consider the alternatives. What about calling? Could you fax or deliver items instead? What about using a videoconferencing center? Don't make a trip if the alternative will be just as effective.

☑ To be more productive on the road, check out portable fax machines, notebook computers, portable printers.

☑ Expect travel delays and plan for them. Allow extra time for driving. Get to the airport earlier. Get boarding passes from your travel agent. Get to the gate at least 30 to 60 minutes before flight time. Don't check luggage. Reserve rental cars ahead of time.

☑ Request a modem-ready hotel room. Bring extension cords for the hotel room. For fewest problems, bring tools to remove wall plates, alligator clips to attach your modem to the phone lines, a line tester to locate live phone lines, and an acoustic coupler to attach to the phone.

☑ Make sure your computer battery is fully charged before you leave. Bring a fully charged replacement battery and an AC adapter cord for your computer. Be sure to take foreign adapters when you travel to other countries.

☑ Use curbside check-in if you must check your luggage.

☑ Check your briefcase before leaving the office. Make sure you have everything you'll need. Don't assume it's already in your briefcase.

☑ To minimize the risk of airsickness, do not eat dairy products or food high in fat or salt less than three hours before you fly. The best way to enjoy the flight is to eat a light, high-carbohydrate meal—whole-grain bread, pasta, fruits, vegetables—2 or 3 hours before take-off.

URGENCY

Sometimes urgent things are important; sometimes they aren't.

☑ When something is urgent, take a little time to think it through. Well-thought-out solutions are usually better than impulsive ones.

☑ Spend your time with the people who are most important to you.

☑ Before you respond, consider the worst that can happen. You are less likely to react emotionally and more likely to respond sensibly.

☑ Urgent and important are not the same thing. See the Priority section.

☑ Most people respond to urgent items far faster than important items. To make important things seem more urgent, set deadlines for them and schedule the activities.

☑ Make time to take care of the important issues, even if they aren't urgent.

VALUE

Calculate the cost
of your time in dollars.

☑ Calculate the cost of your time per minute. It is probably higher than you realize. Be sure to include salary, bonuses, commissions, fringe benefits, expenses, and overhead.

☑ Sometimes it is easier to decide whether or not to do a task if you think of the dollars involved rather than the time involved. Using your personal time-cost per minute, translate the time into dollars. Where as you may be prone to excuse something because it only takes a few minutes, you may think differently when you see what it costs.

☑ Calculate the cost of preparing and distributing all reports. Ask if they're worth what they cost.

☑ Calculate the cost of meetings. Ask if the results are worth what they cost.

☑ Calculate the money cost for any activity, not just the time involved. Many people find it easier to make decisions based on money than on time. Either way, it helps you decide what's really important and worth doing.

VISITORS

Develop criteria for deciding who you should see and who you shouldn't.

☑ Meet visitors outside your office. Hold stand-up conferences in hallways, reception areas, and conference rooms.

☑ Remove extra chairs from your office. Don't keep visitor chairs too close to your desk.

☑ The more comfortable you make visitors, the longer they will stay.

☑ Make sure a clock is visible to your visitors, the larger the better. They will be more aware of time passing and more likely to stick to the point of the visit.

☑ Ask people to make appointments.

☑ Develop a set of criteria for deciding who you will see and who you won't. Just because someone wants part of your time doesn't mean you are obligated to give it to them.

☑ See the section on Drop-Ins.

☑ Keep a record of all your drop-ins for a few days and study the patterns.

VOICE MAIL

You have 17 new messages. To listen to your messages, press 1.

Success with voice mail requires good messages.

☑ Voice mail can be a huge time saver. It lets you share information with people without actually speaking to them. It lets you communicate across different time zones. Messages usually take less time than actual conversations.

☑ Be sure you leave a complete message. According to AT&T, most messages contain only a name and phone number. The more complete the message, the better the other person can help you.

☑ Think about what a good message should include, for example, your name, number, time and day, your company name, the best time to call you, what you need or want.

☑ Be diligent about returning calls as promptly as you can. People will be more likely to leave you messages in the future.

☑ Make sure your voice-mail system allows callers the option of talking to a real person. Do this early in the message.

☑ Tell callers who else they can talk to when you're not in.

☑ Give callers the option of talking to your secretary or leaving you a message on voice mail.

☑ If your voice-mail system allows, increase the playback speed when you listen to your messages.

☑ If you're getting too many calls, try reducing the number of calls your voice-mail box will hold.

☑ Listen to your messages several times during the day. Delete as many as you can; save them only if you really need them.

☑ Make the outgoing message informative, courteous, and brief. Encourage the caller to leave a message.

☑ Use an energetic, enthusiastic voice, and smile when you're recording the message. Take a deep breath before you start, exhale some of it, then start talking. You'll have a much better message, and callers will respond better.

☑ Put the most important information in the beginning of your message.

☑ If you list your phone number at the beginning of your message, repeat it again at the end of your message. This may save having to go back through the message again for the number.

☑ Don't let the phone ring more than once or twice before the voice mail cuts in or callers become irritated.

☑ Don't give callers too many choices, and be sure to keep the choices simple.

☑ Turn on your voice mail periodically so you can concentrate on important work.

WAITING

**Some waiting is inevitable.
Use it well if you can, relax if you can't;
fussing and fuming won't help.**

- ☑ Try to prepare for waiting or try to reduce it. When that doesn't work, accept it. Relax when you're forced to wait. Fussing and fuming won't help and will probably hurt.

- ☑ Consider how to make waiting time productive.

- ☑ Give people complete information the first time. Make sure your instructions are clear.

- ☑ Specify deadlines when requesting action. Jobs without deadlines go to the bottom of the pile.

- ☑ Ask for delivery commitments. Check before the due date to see if there will be any problems meeting them.

- ☑ Confirm appointments and meetings.

- ☑ Start early. Things seem to go your way more often when you get an early start.

☑ Anticipate waiting problems and consider alternatives. Check on any critical details. Double-check and triple-check too.

☑ Some people are notoriously late with everything. When you must deal with them, increase your follow-up efforts.

☑ Be prepared to wait. Take other work with you. If you have to wait you will have something important to do. You might be able to make phone calls or handle some of your paperwork.

☑ Consider waiting as a gift of time. Do something that you had not counted on having the time to do.

☑ Develop the on-time habit. Be on time for appointments and meetings, deliver your work on time, never make others wait for you. Encourage others to develop the on-time habit too.

☑ Use waiting time to work on expense accounts, letters, plans, or reading.

WASTEBASKETS

The art of wastebasketry facilitates productivity.

☑ Get a large wastebasket. The bigger it is, the more you will throw away.

☑ Try to fill your wastebasket every day.

☑ Be sure there is an easily accessible wastebasket in each location where you work.

WRITING

Most writing is to persuade or inform; good writing does this best.

☑ Think before you write. Plan what you want to say. A well-constructed outline may be half the work involved in writing. But start without the outline and you'll spend 3 to 4 times the effort for a finished product.

☑ Many people could write better and quicker if they would try to write like they talk.

☑ Learn to write fewer words and avoid unneeded words. Most people use 3 to 5 times as many words as they need to describe what they're trying to say.

☑ If your writing is quick-and-easy to read, people will read it and respond sooner.

☑ Short sentences and paragraphs are easier to read. Limit sentences to no more than 15 to 20 words. Limit paragraphs to no more than 3 to 4 sentences.

☑ A picture is often faster and better than words. Use graphs, tables, drawings, etc.

☑ Use the Fog Index to check how easy it is to read and understand your writing. (1) Count the number of words. (2) Count the number of sentences. (3) Divide the total words by the number of sentences to get the average words per sentence. (4) Count all words with three or more syllables (big words). (5) Divide the number of big words by the total words to get the percentage of big words. (6) Add the results from step 3 and step 5. (7) Multiply the sum in step 6 by 0.4. (8) This is your Fog Index. If it's higher than 12, you should rewrite your message.

☑ You can also make it quicker for readers if you use devices to guide them through the material, such as **boldface**, *italics*, 1,2,3 numbered sequences, ● round bullets, ■ square bullets, ❑ ballot box bullets, ✷ stars, subheads, Q & A format, sidebars (or boxed material), indented text, color, **different** fonts.

☑ Write for the reader—to express, not to impress. Have someone else check to see how well you've done this.

☑ Use simple, expressive words. Write to gain the reader's understanding, not to impress the reader with your vocabulary.

☑ Try never to use a word with more than two syllables.

☑ To keep letters brief, state your purpose for writing in the first sentence. Not only does it take less time to prepare a short letter but your letter is usually better, too.

☑ When writing long reports, put a summary of the main points in the beginning of the report.

☑ Instead of writing a letter or memo, try using the telephone instead. It's faster and often cheaper.

☑ Use the SOPPADA approach to present your ideas to others. It's fast, it's easy, and it often leads to quicker approval. SOPPADA is an acronym for subject, objective, present situation, proposal, advantages, disadvantages, action.

☑ Using SOPPADA is easy. Subject = what your proposal is about. Objective = what result you plan to achieve. Present Situation = a brief description of current conditions. Proposal = a brief description of the actions necessary to reach your objective. Advantages = why your proposal is a good idea. List only the *three* main advantages; don't go for overkill. Disadvantages = what might go wrong. List the *two* main disadvantages. (There are always at least two disadvantages with even the best proposal: It involves change, and it costs something.) List each disadvantage in two sentences. The first sentence describes the disadvantage. The second sentence begins with the word *However*, followed by a description of how that disadvantage will be overcome. Action = a detailed description of the first action step and who will be responsible for it.

☑ Learn to say more with fewer words. Eliminate unnecessary words, sentences, and paragraphs. There is nothing wrong with one-paragraph letters.

☑ Use simple words rather than complex words; use familiar words.

HERE'S MY *SOPPADA* IDEA!

SUBJECT ....

OBJECTIVE ....

**PRESENT
SITUATION** ....

....

....

....

PROPOSAL ....

....

....

....

....

....

....

....

ADVANTAGES ....

....

....

....

DISADVANTAGES ....

....

....

....

ACTION ....

☑ Don't be lulled into thinking the spell-checker on your computer will do all the work for you. First of all, it doesn't edit your writing. Second, it doesn't even catch all the spelling errors. For example, the spell-checker won't catch correct spelling of proper names, improper words spelled correctly, spelling errors of words not in the computer's dictionary. By all means, use the spell-checker, but don't forget to visually check your writing, too.

☑ Boil down what you want to say and express it in simple declarative sentences. When there is a simpler way to say something, use it.

☑ Using the active voice takes 20 to 30 percent fewer words and produces more impact. The passive voice is lifeless, vague, and wordy. The active voice is dynamic, direct, and takes less time.

☑ Available in any bookstore and worth reading often: *Elements of Style,* by William Strunk and E. B. White (Macmillan Publishing, 5th edition, 1979). First published in the 1920s, this is still the best 78 pages on good writing ever published.

eXTRAS

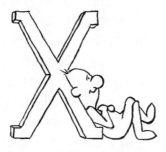

Life is too important to be taken seriously. Learn to laugh at yourself and your circumstances.

☑ Learn to go with the flow of life. Having your own way all the time is really not very important in the grand scheme of things.

☑ Pride and greed are tremendous timewasters. They also destroy relationships and organizations. Learn to avoid them.

☑ Some of the best television programs are on A&E and The Learning Channel. These may even be time well spent.

☑ Take lots of vacations. An increasing number of people spend too much time with their jobs and not enough time away from the job. And when you do get away, don't take any part of the job with you.

☑ Learn to appreciate the simple things in life. Think more about what you have than what you don't.

☑ Look for ways to simplify your life. See the section called Simplifying.

☑ From H. K. Dugdale, here are 50 good ways to use your time to make the most out of your job. Take time to admit and correct your mistakes, answer questions, be careful, be concise, be cooperative, be courteous, be efficient, be enthusiastic, be helpful, be honest, be human, be kind, be neat, be patient, be on time, be thankful, be thorough, be tolerant, build people up, control your temper, develop faith, do it now, do your best, enjoy your family, explain, finish what you start, get the facts, give and take orders cheerfully, improve yourself, learn, listen, live up to your promises, look for the best in people, make friends, make helpful suggestions, make intelligent decisions, make people feel important, plan, praise, pursue a hobby, put first things first, read, relax, remember, save, say thank you, smile, take care of your health, think, understand others, understand yourself.

YOU

Force yourself to become better than you are.

☑ Most of us don't change much unless we're forced to do so. For positive change, force yourself to...

...talk calmly, even though you feel like screaming!

...look for positives, even though all you can see are negatives!

...listen, even though you feel like talking!

...praise the good, even though you feel like criticizing the bad!

...boost people, even though you feel like blaming them!

...ask questions, even though you feel like giving orders and making rules!

...delegate, even though you feel like doing it yourself!

...do it now, even though you feel like putting it off!

...do the important, even though you feel like chasing the urgent!

...think of others first, even though you feel like thinking of yourself first!

...do more, even though you feel like doing less!

...trust others, even though you feel afraid to trust!

...be polite, even though you feel like being rude!

...serve others, even though you feel like being served!

...get better organized, even though you feel like you never could!

...be cheerful, even though you feel like being grumpy!

...forgive, even though you feel like seeking revenge!

...be thankful, even though you feel like complaining!

...be humble, even though you feel boastful and arrogant!

...be a team player, even though you feel like going it alone!

...think more about getting good results than about getting your own way!

...focus on whatever is good and true and noble and honorable!

☑ Take the time to discover more about your temperament. Different temperaments respond differently to time management issues. Learn to understand why you do what you do in the way you do it.

☑ Worth reading: *People Smarts: Bending the Golden Rule to Give Others What They Want* (Pfeiffer, 1994), by Tony Alessandra and Michael O'Connor, with Janice VanDyke.

☑ When you make a promise, keep it. When you say you'll do something, do it. When you promise something by a certain time, deliver it.

☑ Henry Ford said, "Whether you think you can, or whether you think you can't, you're right." The message is clear: Yes you can...if you believe you can!

☑ Choose to be the best you can be every day.

ZANIES

**Use your creativity;
you'll be amazed at the results.**

☑ An old Navajo once asked me why I wore a wristwatch. No matter what I said, he asked, "Why?" I finally got the point and took it off. It helps free you from time compulsion.

☑ To get creative solutions for problems faster and easier, try the Silva water technique. (1) Just before going to bed, fill a glass with water. Close your eyes, turn them slightly upward, and drink half the water while saying to yourself, "This is all I need to do to find the solution to the problem I have in mind (specify the problem)." Then set the glass aside and go to sleep. (2) Sometime during the night, you may wake up from a dream that gives you the answer, or you may remember the dream in the morning. If so, in the morning drink the remaining water and give thanks. (3) If not, drink the remaining water, with your eyes closed and turned up, while mentally repeating, "This is all I need to do to find the solution to the problem I have in mind." You are likely to have a flash of insight during the day. Go ahead, try it. What have you got to lose?

☑ Albert Einstein: "Imagination is more important than knowledge. For while knowledge defines all we currently know and understand, imagination points to all we might yet discover and create...I simply imagine it so, then go about to prove it."

☑ Use your dreams creatively. (1) Place a pad and pencil beside your bed. (2) Tell yourself to think about the situation or problem and to awaken after you've finished your dream. (3) Wake up when the dream is finished, but keep your eyes closed and review the dream. (4) Open your eyes and write down the main elements. (5) Go back to sleep. (6) When you awake, go over your notes and fill in the details. This one has worked for me for several years, and it will probably work for you too. Sure beats wasting time trying to force an answer.

APPENDIX

Dr. Douglass has designed 50 different forms to help you master your time. These forms are available in a master set so you can copy them as much as you like, or you can get all the forms on a diskette for use in your word processing program. However you choose to use them, these forms have all proven valuable resources in helping people master time problems.

To order the master set of forms or the diskette, call or write:

Time Management Center
1401 Johnson Ferry Road, Suite 328
Marietta, Georgia 30062
Telephone: 770-973-3977
Internet: MerrillDouglas@compuserve.com

MEET THE AUTHOR

Dr. Merrill Douglass is a speaker, consultant, and author. He is also a man on a mission. His goal is to change the way people think, work, and live...to help them achieve more productive results and more positive relationships...to achieve greater productivity, increased satisfaction, and a better quality of life.

Since 1972, Dr. Douglass has become an internationally recognized authority in time management and personal productivity. He has presented over 3000 programs and seminars in 36 countries around the world. His clients have included Fortune 500 firms, government agencies, leading universities, trade associations, church organizations, and small- to medium-sized businesses of all kinds. In 1976, Dr. Douglass created the deluxe two-day Time Management seminar for the American Management Association, which became the premiere program of its kind in the United States. Between 1976 and 1996, he presented this program more than 600 times.

There have been many awards and recognitions along the way. The National Speakers Association named him a Certified Speaking Professional in 1983. He received the Sammy Award in Research and Development for creating the unique Time Mastery Profile. *Fortune* magazine and *The Wall Street Journal* have called him a top expert. He has been listed in *Who's Who in America, American Men* and *Women of Science, Who's Who in Finance and Industry,* and *Personalities of the South.*

Dr. Douglass is the author of several books, including *Manage Your Time, Your Work, Yourself; Time Management for Teams;* and *Success Secrets.* His books have been translated into five languages. His cassette tape album, The NEW Time Management, was a best-seller. Dr. Douglass has also written hundreds of articles for magazines and journals, newspaper columns, and daily radio commentaries.

In his consulting and seminar work, Dr. Douglass draws upon a varied background in business and education. He has many years practical experience as a successful manager and entrepreneur and has also been a professor in several universities. He earned his doctorate from Indiana University with a double major in Management and Organizational Behavior.

For more information about seminars or consulting services, please contact Dr. Douglass at:

> Time Management Center
> 1401 Johnson Ferry Road, Suite 328
> Marietta, Georgia 30062
> Telephone 770-973-3977
> Internet MerrillDouglas@compuserve.com